2/2013

TRIATHLON ANATOMY

Mark Klion, MD
Troy Jacobson

Human Kinetics

Library of Congress Cataloging-in-Publication Data

Klion, Mark, 1962-
Triathlon anatomy / Mark Klion, Troy Jacobson.
p. cm.
1. Triathlon--Training. 2. Triathletes--Physiology. I. Jacobson, Troy. II. Title.
GV1060.73.K55 2012
796.42'57--dc23
2012028408

ISBN-10: 1-4504-2138-5 (print)
ISBN-13: 978-1-4504-2138-6 (print)

This publication is written and published to provide accurate and authoritative information relevant to the subject matter presented. It is published and sold with the understanding that the author and publisher are not engaged in rendering legal, medical, or other professional services by reason of their authorship or publication of this work. If medical or other expert assistance is required, the services of a competent professional person should be sought.

The web addresses cited in this text were current as of August 2012, unless otherwise noted.

Acquisitions Editor: Tom Heine; **Developmental Editor:** Cynthia McEntire; **Assistant Editor:** Elizabeth Evans; **Copyeditor:** Patricia L. MacDonald; **Permissions Manager:** Martha Gullo; **Graphic Designer:** Fred Starbird; **Graphic Artist:** Julie L. Denzer; **Cover Designer:** Keith Blomberg; **Photographer (for interior illustration references):** Neil Bernstein; **Photographer (for cover illustration reference):** Dieter Nagl/ AFP/Getty Images; **Photo Asset Manager:** Laura Fitch; **Visual Production Assistant:** Joyce Brumfield; **Art Manager:** Kelly Hendren; **Associate Art Manager:** Alan L. Wilborn; **Illustrator (cover and interior):** Jen Gibas; **Printer:** Versa Press

Human Kinetics books are available at special discounts for bulk purchase. Special editions or book excerpts can also be created to specification. For details, contact the Special Sales Manager at Human Kinetics.

Printed in the United States of America   10 9 8 7 6 5 4 3 2 1

The paper in this book is certified under a sustainable forestry program.

Human Kinetics
Website: www.HumanKinetics.com

United States: Human Kinetics
P.O. Box 5076
Champaign, IL 61825-5076
800-747-4457
e-mail: humank@hkusa.com

Canada: Human Kinetics
475 Devonshire Road Unit 100
Windsor, ON N8Y 2L5
800-465-7301 (in Canada only)
e-mail: info@hkcanada.com

Europe: Human Kinetics
107 Bradford Road
Stanningley
Leeds LS28 6AT, United Kingdom
+44 (0) 113 255 5665
e-mail: hk@hkeurope.com

Australia: Human Kinetics
57A Price Avenue
Lower Mitcham, South Australia 5062
08 8372 0999
e-mail: info@hkaustralia.com

New Zealand: Human Kinetics
P.O. Box 80
Torrens Park, South Australia 5062
0800 222 062
e-mail: info@hknewzealand.com

E5611

I would like to dedicate this book to my loving wife, Jennifer, and children, Jack, Rebecca, and Kyle, who constantly support me in all of my endeavors. Without their love and understanding I would not be the person I am today. I love you.

Mark Klion

This book is dedicated to my beautiful daughters, Hope and Chloe. May your dreams become your reality. Special thanks to my parents for their unconditional support over the years and to Jen, for her ongoing strength and inspiration in all that I do.

Troy Jacobson

CONTENTS

PREFACE

Triathlon participation has grown significantly over the last 10 years. Technology has paved the way for advances in almost every aspect of training and racing. Every year improvements in equipment are promoted as making an athlete go faster, look better, and stay healthy while participating in the sport of triathlon. These improvements all come with a price tag. For the beginner triathlete, these technological advancements can be of less importance than the simple joy of participating and fulfilling a goal of race completion.

Triathlon training and racing are not activities we all grew up with. The days of Little League games, travel soccer, and the many other individual and team sports we might have participated in and those that many active weekend warriors now enjoy do not lend themselves as a natural transition to the rigors of triathlon participation. There are rare cases of people, including professional and age-group competitive racers, who are highly experienced in all three disciplines. Today, through increased involvement of adolescent and younger children in triathlon participation, a new breed of athletes is being developed who may have a better chance of being great at all three. Oh, to be young again!

Triathlon is considered by some to have its beginnings in France in the 1920s. The first modern swim, bike, run event to be called a triathlon was held at Mission Bay, San Diego, California, on September 25, 1974. Since then races at every distance imaginable, from sprint, Olympic, half Ironman, full Ironman, and Decaman—10 Ironmans all at once—are run almost every weekend in the United States and worldwide.

Whatever the distance may be, the principles of training remain the same. Improved cardiorespiratory fitness and increased musculoskeletal strength and power build the foundation of improved performance. Triathletes often like to say, "The larger the engine, the faster the train." A fast engine that breaks down frequently from overtraining can be problematic and frustrating. A well-thought-out training program that includes strength and flexibility training can create a large engine that runs smoothly.

As an athlete commits more time and effort to the sport, injury prevention and often injury management can be crucial. The information presented in this book allows both novice and experienced athletes to obtain a better understanding of how the musculoskeletal system functions and responds to triathlon-specific exercises and training. Remember to never stray far from the fundamentals of safe and effective endurance sports training for performance.

The first chapter introduces the triathlon world. This is followed by a discussion of the effects of exercise on the cardiovascular and cardiorespiratory systems, which make up the engine. Chapters 4 through 10 provide detailed anatomical descriptions and pictorial explanations of sport-specific exercises that have been shown to improve strength and performance. Every exercise includes a code that represents the three disciplines of triathlon participation. Some exercises will be more specific for one or more sports. Use the symbols to guide your specific training program so it addresses both potential weaknesses and strengths in training and racing. This will be helpful in chapter 3 on how to customize a training plan. Chapter 11 provides essential information on injury prevention, with a description of common injuries triathletes encounter as well as appropriate exercises and treatment principles to help an athlete get back on track.

One unique feature of *Triathlon Anatomy* we hope you find helpful is the anatomical drawings accompanying the description of each exercise. They illustrate key muscles used during each movement, using color to distinguish engagement of primary and secondary muscle groups, from start to completion.

 Primary muscles   Secondary muscles

Participation in triathlons is a commitment to health and fitness. For some athletes, racing is the pinnacle prize, but for many people, triathlon becomes a lifestyle enriched with training, racing, and a community that thrives on sharing information. This book contains pearls of wisdom that are learned only through experience. Sharing them with you will hopefully help you maintain a consistent and healthful life in triathlon participation. Train smart and stay healthy.

THE TRIATHLETE IN MOTION

The need for speed is not a new concept. Human's desire to go faster dates back many thousands of years from the first Olympiad to the recent title of the fastest man on earth. The modern version of the sport of triathlon is barely 40 years old but has undergone an incredible evolution. From the first triathlon in 1974 to the inaugural Ironman-distance triathlon, which had only 15 competitors, who could have imagined this would become an international phenomenon? The desire for triathlon participation continues to grow, and as most experienced triathletes know and newbies quickly learn, many if not all of the popular races that become available for online entry sell out within minutes. Whether this is good or bad for the sport has yet to be determined. It does speak to the incredible appetite and attraction for triathlon participation.

USA Triathlon, the national governing body of the sport in the United States, saw its membership numbers grow by 523 percent over 10 years, from 21,341 in 2000 to 133,000 in 2010, according to the Sporting Goods Manufacturers Association. The latest data show that more than 2.3 million people participated in a triathlon. Needless to say, there is a boom in triathlon as a sport.

As the saying goes, "If you build it, they will come," and so has the triathlon generation. Every sport has a signature event. Many runners look to the marathon either as an ultimate goal or something that would be if only they could find the right knees to run it. Cyclists often dream of being in the Tour de France, holding a glass of champagne, riding along with their teammates, being saluted by the fans. Mountain bikers covet the Leadville Trail 100. For the avid runner, it's the Boston Marathon. Swimmers may dream of being at the Olympic trials or swimming the English Channel. For many triathletes the lure of an Ironman, especially the Kona Ironman World Championships, captivates their imaginations. For a relatively few people these dreams become a reality, but for others it may suffice just to be part of a community of similar souls. Triathlon participation becomes one of their identities. This community has seen significant growth in numbers over the years but has also created an industry that caters to the very needs of its constituents.

Technological advancements in equipment are revealed every month in triathlon publications. Articles on training techniques, injury prevention, nutrition, and almost every imaginable subject as it applies to the sport of triathlon are available to the inquisitive triathlete. Triathlon clubs are sprouting in every community. These clubs often provide training partners, coaching services, discounts on purchases, and a feeling of incredible camaraderie. With all these resources available to athletes, it is no wonder many are able to swim faster, bike stronger, run faster, and of course look fashionable while doing it.

Triathlon Distances

No matter the distance, a triathlon is a multisport event involving the completion of three activities in succession, usually swimming, biking, and running. Races of every distance are available and accessible to all takers. Common distances are Sprint, Olympic (or International), half Ironman (or IM 70.3), and full Ironman (table 1.1).

Table 1.1 Triathlon Distances

	Swim	Bike	Run
Sprint	750 m	20K	5K
Olympic	1,500 m	40K	10K
Half Ironman	1.2 mi	56 mi	13.1 mi
Full Ironman	2.4 mi	112 mi	26.2 mi

Sprint triathlons and other races of shorter distances can be attractive to beginner triathletes as the time commitment to training can be less. Also some athletes simply excel at shorter distances and enjoy high-intensity, all-out racing. The duration of a sprint triathlon can vary, but usually a time of 1 hour and 20 minutes is considered competitive, depending on the age group.

At the Olympic distance, training and racing times correspondingly increase. According to race director John Korff, the average finishing time of more than 3,500 athletes at the New York City Olympic-distance triathlon for 2010 was 3:04:39. The winner recorded a time of 1:48:11!

Training time and race duration continue to climb for half-Ironman and Ironman distances. Despite the ease of the metric system, these races are often better described in miles. A half Ironman is now often referred to as a 70.3, reflecting the overall completed distance of the race. The Ironman distance or 140.6 is a 2.4-mile swim followed by 112 miles on the bike, finishing with a 26.2-mile run. The Ironman continues to be the holy grail for some athletes and attracts competitors of every age, size, and ability.

Transitions

Between each leg of the triathlon is a transition from one activity to another. T1 and T2, as they are called, are transitions from swimming to biking and biking to running, respectively. Veteran triathletes know that the time to complete these transitions also needs to be calculated into the overall finishing time. Races can be won or lost in the transition area. It is not a place for lounging. Transitions can also play a critical role in race recovery, a moment to rest, and management of issues, including nutritional needs, sunscreen application, and bathroom breaks, that occur during a race.

Biomechanics of Triathlon

Triathlon participation involves three activities: swimming, biking, and running. Each activity requires a coordinated pattern of muscle recruitment that produces motion about the joints and creates the power to make the triathlete move. As a triathlete transitions from one discipline to the next, a concomitant increase in weight-bearing activity is seen.

The swim requires the triathlete to be prone, lying facedown in the water and using the arms and legs for propulsion. Most people without a swimming background quickly learn that swimming efficiency and, thus, speed are extremely dependent on technique. For those who are technically challenged, wetsuits, which are legal to use in certain water temperatures, provide buoyancy to help produce better swimming position, resulting in less drag on the legs. Most triathletes use the arms to a much greater extent than the lower extremities for propulsion, possibly to prevent lower-extremity fatigue when biking and running.

The transition to the bike places a greater emphasis on both the lower extremities and core. The upper extremities contribute stabilization and assist in bike-handling skills.

Running, the greatest weight-bearing activity of the three, places the most impact on the body and requires a smooth coordination between upper and lower extremities to enable efficient gait. Strength training with both isolated and sport-specific exercises as described in later chapters will help develop a strong foundation to create power and speed and also prevent injury.

A Test of Endurance

The common thread that binds all triathlon distances together is that they all require prolonged exercise tolerance. This is unlike many other sports. Professional American football players play an average of 12 minutes during a 60-minute game. It has been calculated that during an average soccer game that lasts 90 minutes, a soccer player runs about 6 miles (10 km). At even the shortest triathlon distance, the ability to maintain sustained exercise needs to be greater.

The cardiorespiratory and musculoskeletal systems can be trained to handle this endurance stress. As more information is learned through research about an athlete's ability to perform both aerobic and anaerobic exercise as well as techniques to improve musculoskeletal function including strength and flexibility training, true athletic performance can be achieved.

Injury prevention and management continue to be a significant component of triathlon participation. Repetitive stresses on the body can cause tissue breakdown and subsequent injury. A broken engine doesn't go very fast. Along with injury management comes a psychological component of training and racing that includes learning to sustain efforts or, as some veterans like to say, to suffer. Digging deep remains an important determinant of performance in endurance sport competition. Some people seem able to push harder and longer, but for most triathletes, the stress of digging deep sometimes does not compare with the pressure of balancing family and work with the rigors of training and racing. The terms *triathlon widow* and *triathlon widower* are not uncommon among those in the triathlon community. For all that is said in jest, this stress, along with the commitment to a healthy life, can seem somewhat overwhelming to new triathletes. After finishing a triathlon of any distance, the elation and celebration often are shared by all those who supported the effort and are well worth the commitment.

Training Considerations

With all the knowledge and gear at our fingertips, why don't we all train and race like the pros? Genetics plays a significant role in a person's athletic ability. Some have the athletic genes, and some don't. Personal commitment and a well-thought-out training program can help an athlete improve performance.

As the knowledge base of human physiology increases, we learn that our bodies respond to a well-planned training program. Training haphazardly or disregarding warning signs of common injuries will cause the body to break down. Every athlete has a threshold beyond which the body begins to break down and the risk of injury increases. That threshold varies from athlete to athlete and also depends on triathlon experience.

The training philosophy of quantity versus quality regarding volume and types of workouts has changed over the years. This is especially true for maturing athletes, those over 40. We all like to think we are still kids and able to train with reckless abandon, but no matter what our age, our bodies can remind us differently with aches, pains, and potential injury if we don't pay attention to our well-being. Endurance capabilities peak at around age 35 and progressively decline until about age 50, after which they decline more significantly. Muscle mass peaks in the mid 20s and progressively declines each year. Sorry for the bad news. On the positive side, science also shows that exercises focusing on increasing strength can reduce this muscle loss. The loss of flexibility, which also accompanies increasing age, can be altered with stretching exercises that help maintain function and reduce injuries. Endurance training for the mature athlete requires this special attention and a lot of tender loving care to sustain a consistent training and racing schedule.

Controversy does exist as to whether strength training actually improves performance. Any coach or sports medicine physician will support a well-outlined training program that includes both strength and flexibility training. The goal of the program should be to promote musculoskeletal health and improve the body's ability to withstand the repetitive stresses placed on it by endurance activities. The development of strength with sport-specific exercises as outlined throughout this book also improves economy of motion, or the ease with which you perform an activity. This will help you go faster and decrease stress on the body.

Core stability, a concept that has become the new buzzword with regard to performance training, can be defined as the body's foundation for movement and power generation. The core muscles of the abdomen and pelvis are an untapped source of stability and power. Weaknesses in that region can be the primary reason for injuries seen in triathlon participation. Strengthening this group as described in chapter 7 can help increase power and speed in all three activities of triathlon participation.

Throughout the book are explanations of how each body part works with respect to triathlon participation. The interactions of the soft tissues, including muscles, tendons, and ligaments, as well as bones and specific joints, are described. Each chapter is a guide to how to best strengthen those areas for increased performance and injury prevention. The exercises described are sport specific. Common injury signs are discussed and the importance of recovery and rest are reinforced to ensure injury-free years of triathlon participation. Chapter 11 provides insight on organizing and implementing a training program to help you remain injury free. In chapter 2, we examine the cardiovascular and cardiorespiratory systems as they relate to triathlon participation. The pumping heart supplies the blood to the muscles as we race and train. The bigger the engine, the stronger the heart and the longer and faster we can go. Train hard but train smart.

CARDIO TRAINING

Why do we exercise? Is it for a better-looking body? To help reduce the stress in our lives? To feel a sense of accomplishment? Yes, all these, and the list can go on and on. From a medical standpoint, research has shown that people who participate in regular exercise programs, including 30 minutes of moderate exercise each day, have remarkably reduced risks of cardiovascular disease, non-insulin-dependent diabetes, high blood pressure, osteoporosis, and colon cancer. For some people, these accomplishments are just what the doctor ordered.

Some triathletes may consider these benefits to be less important than the prime goal of getting faster and going longer. For triathletes, building the biggest and strongest engine is what training is about. This chapter helps develop an understanding of how improvements to the cardiovascular and cardiorespiratory systems can help build the engine and improve health and performance.

Cardiovascular and Cardiorespiratory Systems

The cardiovascular and cardiorespiratory systems (figure 2.1), which include the heart, arteries, capillaries, and veins, along with the lungs and their vasculature, support and enable five important functions required for exercise:

1. The heart delivers oxygen to the working muscles via the arteries.
2. The blood returns to the lungs via the veins to be reoxygenated.
3. The heat generated by the working muscles is transported to the skin via arteries and capillaries to help regulate the body temperature.
4. Glucose (for energy) and hormones (for homeostasis) are transported to active tissues via the bloodstream.
5. Metabolic wastes are transported away from the active tissues via the veins and lymphatic vessels to allow continued activity.

Heart Delivers Oxygen to Working Muscles

The heart, which is a muscle, responds to exercise by increasing its size and thus can increase force of contraction. In doing so it is able to efficiently pump more blood to the working muscles. Cardiac output (CO), the amount of blood pushed into the arteries in a given time period, is a medical measure used to determine heart function; the higher the number, the stronger the heart. It is often calculated with this equation:

CO = stroke volume (amount of blood pushed with each contraction) × heart rate

Exercise-induced cardiac benefits include a decrease in resting, exercising, and recovery heart rates. Resting heart rate can be used to measure athletic recovery and overall health status. To measure resting heart rate, take your heart rate after waking up while still lying in bed without moving. A variation of as few as five beats above normal can be an indication of impending illness or potential overtraining. Exercising heart rate is taken manually

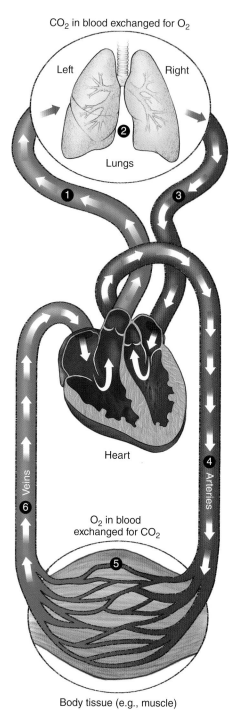

CO$_2$ in blood exchanged for O$_2$

Left　　　Right

❷

Lungs

❶　　　❸

Heart

❹ Arteries

Veins

❻

O$_2$ in blood exchanged for CO$_2$

❺

Body tissue (e.g., muscle)

Figure 2.1　The blood circulates through the heart, lungs, and muscles.

during a workout or with a heart rate monitor. A better-conditioned athlete will be able to swim, run, or bike at a lower heart rate, producing a lower metabolic demand. Another benefit of a strong heart is a decrease in the time it takes the heart rate to return to a resting level after exercise, known as the recovery rate. Medical research shows that people who have a decrease of less than 12 beats in the first minute after exercise may be at risk for cardiovascular disease.

Some other measures important for assessing physiological fitness include maximum heart rate, lactate threshold, and $\dot{V}O_2$max. These should be assessed with appropriate equipment and in the presence of a trained person who can best interpret the results.

For this discussion, $\dot{V}O_2$max is defined as a person's maximum capacity to transport and use oxygen. This concept relies on the ability to deliver oxygen to the tissues and then use it for energy production. Many conditions can affect $\dot{V}O_2$max, including lung disease, which decreases oxygen diffusion to the blood; a weak heart that can't pump blood to the tissues; and untrained muscles, which don't have the cellular tools to process the oxygen. Although it is often considered the single best measure of cardiorespiratory fitness and maximal aerobic power, $\dot{V}O_2$max is often a very bad predictor of performance. $\dot{V}O_2$max values are affected by many other variables including age, sex, body weight, fitness level, and individual genetic factors. For most trained athletes, $\dot{V}O_2$max values change by as little as 10 percent with training. The greatest gains are seen in people who are untrained and start an exercise program.

What appears to be somewhat more accurate in determining performance is an athlete's ability to swim, bike, or run at or close to $\dot{V}O_2$max for a given period of time. This is referred to as percent $\dot{V}O_2$max and relates to a concept called anaerobic threshold, or lactate threshold, the point at which lactate production exceeds the body's ability to process it, and performance cannot be maintained. More is discussed later in the chapter. Through aerobic workouts that increase the cellular machinery to process oxygen and through lactate threshold workouts to help develop better exercise tolerance, athletes can build a bigger and more efficient engine. (This is discussed further in chapter 3.)

Blood Returns to Lungs

In the blood returned to the heart, the red blood cells have been depleted of available oxygen. A protein called hemoglobin, which makes up the majority of a red blood cell, binds oxygen and allows it to be transported to muscles and internal organs. The lungs and their capillaries replenish the red-cell oxygen deficit. The percentage of red blood cells in whole blood, called the hematocrit level, is normally 45 percent in men and 40 percent in women. The other components in blood include plasma, which is mostly water; dissolved proteins; glucose; clotting factors; minerals; hormones; and carbon dioxide.

Altitude training has been touted for its beneficial effects on cardiorespiratory training because inspired air that has a reduced level of oxygen can induce increases in red blood cell production and thus increase oxygen-carrying capacity. However, the concept "train high, race low" has been challenged in the last few years and remains controversial. This process of acclimatization, which can include increases in red blood cell numbers under the hormonal control of erythropoietin, may take as long as 4 weeks to occur. Training at altitudes above certain levels can actually be detrimental to performance and cardiorespiratory function. A more reasonable altitude training program is to sleep at high altitude or use an oxygen tent to stimulate the production of red blood cells, then train and race at low altitude. Other methods used to increase the production of red blood cells, such as using performance-enhancing drugs or blood transfusions, are illegal and can be very dangerous.

Heat Transported to Skin for Temperature Regulation

Thermoregulation, the ability to keep the core body temperature within certain boundaries, is accomplished by heat loss from convection, conduction, radiation, and evaporation. Heat-related illnesses can affect performance and, in severe cases, even cause death. As the body's internal organs and muscles are worked through exercise, heat is generated and core temperature can rise. Radiation and conduction loss occurs when the skin temperature is warmer than the outside temperature. Production and evaporation of sweat also facilitate heat loss. As body temperature rises, the smaller arteries, the arterioles, that supply the skin dilate and redirect blood flow to the capillary beds of the skin to increase heat loss by convection and conduction. This is classically seen in the red flush that athletes develop around the face, chest, and arms during exercise. Factors such as humidity, wind, and clothing can significantly alter an athlete's ability to control heat loss.

Heat-related illnesses may occur at any level of triathlon participation. The average normal body temperature is 98.6 degrees Fahrenheit (37 °C). Hyperthermia, a state in which the core temperature increases because of failed thermoregulation, is defined as a temperature of 100 to 101 degrees Fahrenheit (37.8 to 38.3 °C). Symptoms include nausea, vomiting, headache, and low blood pressure, which can lead to dizziness and fainting. If left untreated, heat stroke, a temperature in excess of 104 degrees Fahrenheit (40 °C), can be fatal. Tips to prevent the negative effects of heat include properly hydrating with cool liquids, wearing a visor or hat to provide shade from the sun, and pouring water on the body or ice on the head to increase conduction loss.

Blood Transports Glucose and Hormones to Active Tissues

The terms *aerobic exercise* and *anaerobic exercise* describe whether cellular metabolism occurs in the presence (aerobic) or absence (anaerobic) of oxygen. At the training level, this can be translated based on the intensity and duration of exercise. Aerobic exercise, such as a long, slow run, is performed at a relatively low intensity for a longer time and in the presence of oxygen for energy production. Anaerobic exercise, such as weightlifting or sprinting, is of short duration and high intensity, and it is performed without the use of oxygen for energy production. During exercise, an active balance between these two processes creates a constant flow of energy to the working muscles.

Muscle contraction and, thus, force generation depend on the availability of energy. One obvious source of energy is the food we eat. Initially, food is digested in the stomach and passed through the small and large intestines for absorption. Carbohydrate is taken up by muscles and the liver and converted to glycogen for storage. The liver stores the most glycogen; when called upon, the liver can rapidly convert glycogen back to glucose to be transported to muscle via blood.

Fats are stored as adipose tissue in the peripheral aspects of the body and have to be broken down in a complex series of steps to a simpler form of glycerol and free fatty acids to be used as energy. Stored fats represent a substantial energy reservoir, but because of slow mobilization and conversion to usable energy forms, energy production from fat is too slow for very intense exercise.

Proteins also provide energy for prolonged exercise but, similar to fats, require an initial breakdown into amino acids that can be utilized in aerobic metabolism. This represents only 5 to 10 percent of total energy expended during endurance exercise. Proteins do play a major role in the response to exercise, including building new tissue such as muscle and repairing tissues damaged from injury or even intense exercise.

The hormonal system responds to exercise by producing endorphins, which can create the runner's high, and testosterone and growth hormone, which promote muscle growth and injury healing. Excessive exercise and overtraining, on the other hand, can stimulate cortisol production that can suppress the immune system, which may lead to illness and loss of training time.

A practical consideration of nutrition and energy production is the ability of the organs to digest and absorb nutrients in the gastrointestinal system during exercise. Blood essential for digestion is shunted away from the gut to provide more blood flow to working muscles. This slows the rate at which the stomach empties into the intestines and can cause symptoms such as bloating, nausea, and vomiting. Excessive caloric intake through too many gels, bars, or even concentrated replacement drinks can exacerbate this condition. If these symptoms are not addressed with reduced exercise intensity or cessation or reduction of nutrient ingestion, significant gastrointestinal distress can occur. Hydrating with plain water for a short period to flush the system and avoiding solid foods during a race can sometimes alleviate some of these symptoms.

Salt loss is also a consideration when discussing gastrointestinal distress. It is hard to quantify salt loss, but if you have ever noticed people who have a white film on their clothes after a race, most likely they sweat salt excessively. Salt is essential to the body, and its balance is crucial for sustained exercise. Replacement can come from drinks or salt tablets taken as supplements as well as from the chicken soup available at the aid stations of endurance triathlons.

Metabolic Wastes Moved Away From Active Tissues

In the first 2 minutes of high-intensity exercise, anaerobic metabolism is the main source of energy production. In this process, glucose is converted to lactate without the presence of oxygen. As exercise continues, aerobic metabolism provides continued energy production. If exercise intensity remains high, lactate production also continues until the body is unable to metabolize it or clear it from the muscles. This is referred to as the lactate threshold. Lactate often is mistakenly referred to as lactic acid and thought to be responsible for muscle fatigue and the burning sensation associated with high-burst exercise. Current research suggests these symptoms are due to acidosis, a change in muscle pH, caused by hydrogen ion production during anaerobic metabolism. Plasma, the other major component of blood, is the medium that carries these metabolic waste products away from active tissues and helps maintain muscle pH balance. An athlete's lactate threshold and percent $\dot{V}O_2$max are useful measures when deciding exercise intensity for training and racing and assessing athletic performance in endurance sports. How long can an athlete sustain high-intensity activity in relation to maximal aerobic capacity? That is the million dollar question!

Heart Rate Training

Similar to the motor in a race car that powers the vehicle, the heart is the motor of the triathlete. Some people are blessed with high-performance V8 turbos, while others are born with four-cylinders. Genetics plays a huge role in one's potential as an endurance athlete, but the good news is we can all improve the output of our engines through proper development and execution of a training plan.

Measuring the output of your motor and training in ideally suited training zones can be done by using a heart rate monitor. Just as a car's tachometer measures the rpms and helps the driver know when to shift gears, a heart rate monitor measures the relative intensity of exercise.

It is important to note that heart rate training, although an effective tool, is not an exact science. Heart rate can be affected by a number of external variables ranging from temperature to your current state of health. Many athletes use heart rate training as a gauge or as an intensity governor of sorts and adjust training intensity accordingly based on how they're feeling.

The first step in using a heart rate monitor effectively is to determine training zones. This can be done by performing a simple field test in training, at a race, or in a lab setting. Each method has its pros and cons, but each can be an effective means of establishing performance benchmarks and training zones.

A variety of popular field tests are available for the triathlete to perform in each sport discipline. One of the simplest and most effective for the bike and the run is the 20-minute threshold test.

20-Minute Threshold Test

1. Warm up for 10 to 20 minutes or until you feel ready to increase the intensity.
2. Perform a few openers—short high-intensity repetitions of 15 to 30 seconds with the same rest period, such as 30 seconds hard and 30 seconds rest.
3. On a repeatable course with limited variables such as stop signs or excessive traffic to interrupt the effort, perform a very hard but sustainable 20-minute effort at your best possible pace for that duration. Remember, pacing is important, so don't start out too hard. Take your average heart rate during the 20-minute effort as your result for the test.
4. Cool down for 10 to 20 minutes.

Once you have this information, you can feel confident that you have discovered your approximate lactate threshold heart rate (LTHR) intensity range within a margin of error of a few percentage points. This number will be important in setting up your target zones (table 2.1).

Table 2.1   Heart Rate Training Zones Based on Lactate Threshold Heart Rate (LTHR)

Zone	Description	Training use	Heart rate ranges
1	Easy	Warm up	60 to 70% of LTHR
2	Moderate	Develop aerobic capacity	70 to 90% of LTHR
3	Difficult	Develop aerobic endurance (LTHR)	90 to 100% of LTHR
4	Very difficult	Increase aerobic economy	100 to 110% of LTHR
5	Extremely difficult	Develop speed and power	110% of LTHR to peak

For example, if your LTHR is 150, your range for zone 1 is 90 to 105 beats per minute (bpm), your range for zone 2 is 105 to 135 bpm, for zone 3 is 135 to 150 bpm, for zone 4 is 150 to 165 bpm, and for zone 5 is 165 bpm to your peak heart rate. For triathlon training, you primarily will work in zones 2 and 3 to develop aerobic capacity and endurance. (See chapter 3 for more on creating a training program.)

Once you have determined your zones either by doing a field test or by getting tested at a human performance lab, you'll be able to train your energy systems in a more effective manner in order to build your engine.

Compression Garments

No cardiovascular discussion can be complete without mentioning compression garments. It's been suggested that using compression garments as recovery aids during exercise may decrease muscle fatigue, improve recovery, and lead to better endurance and performance. Some of these benefits pertain to their effects on the cardiovascular system. Unfortunately most have not been scientifically validated.

Unlike arteries, veins have no significant pump pushing blood back to the heart and lungs. Muscle action provides some propulsive force. One-way valves in veins stop backflow caused by gravity. It is in this low-flow system that wastes from cellular activity are returned toward the heart and lungs. Venous insufficiency is a condition in which the veins of the lower extremities are unable to facilitate efficient blood return to the heart. Veins become congested, creating varicose veins in the legs and perhaps causing pain and swelling. This can occur from genetic predisposition, pregnancy, and possibly standing for long periods. Endurance racing may also contribute to this problem, and compression garments may assist flow and prevent or treat lower-extremity swelling, pain, and varicose veins.

The cardiovascular and cardiorespiratory systems that make up the engine that drives the body are just one piece of the puzzle in improving health and fitness. The effect of exercise on these two systems is an extremely complex topic that is continually updated and better understood. In the next chapter, you will discover the best way to develop an effective training program. In the remaining chapters, you will learn the exercises that build the apparatus. The end result will be better speed and strength as well as injury prevention.

CHAPTER 3

CREATING A CUSTOMIZED TRAINING PLAN

Before we dive into training program design, we want you to have a clear understanding of training principles to help you approach your performance potential. Whereas exercise can be loosely defined as random physical activity for the purpose of improving fitness, training can be defined as exercising with structure with the goal of successful completion of an event. To maximize your time and energy as well as to reach your performance goals, training regimens should be purposeful and structured, leading to the accomplishment of short-range and long-range goals.

Training Terms and Principles

This chapter covers some terms and principles used by coaches and athletes. Every athlete should be familiar with these concepts.

Periodization of Training

Periodization is defined as varying training volume and intensity in distinct cycles over a period of time in preparation to peak for a goal event. The two types of exercise periodization are linear and nonlinear. In linear periodization, the athlete exclusively targets one energy system or training focus over the course of a microcycle of 4 to 6 weeks, progressing from lower- to higher-intensity work with each cycle. In nonlinear periodization, the athlete uses various energy systems and intensities throughout a training cycle, developing them simultaneously. Both methods have their staunch supporters and critics, although many coaches today lean toward the nonlinear periodization model because of its apparent ability to produce results while helping prevent overtraining and injury, which are common in the linear method, by jumping from one plane of intensity to the next.

Workload

For endurance athletes, workload is measured in terms of frequency, duration, and intensity of exercise. Frequency of training refers to the number of bouts of specific exercise per cycle, whether a week, month, or year. Duration is the length of the training session. Intensity is how hard the work is performed. These parameters are manipulated during the course of a training program to achieve the desired result of enhanced performance.

Recovery and Adaptation

Just as overall workload is an important concept to understand, so is recovery and adaptation. In simple terms, the human body adapts to the stresses of training during rest and becomes stronger in order to handle a similar workload again in the future. You must consider the training adaptation cycle when you are designing and executing a training plan. Lack of emphasis on recovery and adaptation often leads to injury and overtraining.

Aerobic Metabolism

Endurance-based athletic events in which pacing is of particular importance, from running a 5K to doing an Ironman triathlon, are primarily grounded in aerobic metabolism. Aerobic metabolism uses an efficient energy production pathway that converts carbohydrate and fat to fuel in order to power movement. Scientists, coaches, and athletes have discovered that exercising at low to moderate intensities does the most good in improving long-distance endurance, in terms of both cardiorespiratory and muscular systems.

Anaerobic Metabolism

Essentially, anaerobic means "without oxygen" and is a less efficient energy pathway when it comes to producing movement. As exercise intensity increases, there's a subtle yet noticeable shift in the body to using carbohydrate as a primary source of fuel. This shift is accompanied by the sensation of burning in the working muscles as well as an increased breathing rate. Exercise at this intensity or higher is short lived, but athletes and coaches understand that the higher the anaerobic threshold becomes through proper training, the faster athletes will be able to go at most intensity levels.

Functional Strength Development

Development of functional strength is very popular in the fitness industry and can be defined as training to enhance the coordinated working relationship between the nervous and muscular systems. Functional training exercises use everyday movement patterns such as standing, twisting, bending, lifting, jumping, walking, and running and are in contrast to exercises that isolate joints. An example is the walking lunge (page 131) versus the leg extension (page 140). Whereas the leg extension isolates the muscles of the quadriceps and makes them stronger, the walking lunge targets all the muscles associated with the fluid movement patterns of standing, walking, and running. A balanced resistance training program will typically have both types of movements as part of the routine.

Interval Training

Interval training, defined as performing a high-intensity burst of effort followed by a period of recovery for varying repetitions, is popular among competitive athletes for its ability to improve cardiorespiratory fitness as well as muscular strength and endurance. Interval training typically targets the anaerobic energy system and improves the athlete's ability to sustain a higher level of output and perform at higher levels of speed for longer durations. An example of an interval session for a cyclist is as follows:

Warm up for 5 to 10 minutes

Cycle 5 × 2 minutes hard at lactate threshold heart rate intensity, with 1 minute recovery in between

Cool down for 5 to 10 minutes

Lactate threshold is a metabolic state the athlete reaches during high-intensity exercise in which lactate accumulates in the blood until it can no longer be removed as efficiently as it is during lower-intensity aerobic exercise.

Long Steady Distance Training

A contrast to interval training, long steady distance training (also known by many as long slow distance training) was popularized by marathon runners in the 1970s. The idea was to develop cardiorespiratory and muscular endurance by incorporating training runs of 1 hour or longer, performed at a pace 1 to 3 minutes slower than marathon pace (i.e., conversational pace) several days a week with at least one longer workout of around 2 hours in duration. Long steady distance training is still a staple training method of many top endurance athletes today, and when combined with a proper dose of interval training, it elicits strong gains in endurance sports performance.

Training Plan Development

There is a lot of science behind optimal training plan development for triathletes. As multisport participation becomes more popular, the research literature on best practices and training methodologies expands at a staggering rate. Although the science of effective training is certainly important, so is the art of developing a training plan.

Triathlon coaching has been an area of explosive growth over the past decade. A range of professional triathlon coaching certifications is now available, and scores of coaching companies, large and small, have sprung up to meet the growing demands of this burgeoning field. Developing a multisport training plan can be daunting, and as athletes attempt to train effectively for three sports, they discover that a knowledgeable coach can save them time and headaches by shortening the learning curve. But although coaching does involve the science of training, it's also important not to neglect the art of training an athlete. After all, if human performance improvement was as simple as adding 1 and 1 to equal 2, everyone would be getting faster and competing at a similar level. The truth is that each athlete is an experiment of one, and a good coach will discover the balance of training in order to help the athlete reach his goals while remaining healthy and injury free. Hence, the art of training.

In many ways, a triathlon coach is like a chef. Every chef has access to common ingredients. It's how they mix, prepare, and then present the ingredients to create the dish that matters. And let's face it: Some dishes are great while others are not so great. It's the same with triathlon coaching and how the coach works with the athlete, addressing individual strengths and weaknesses in order to develop the ideal program for achieving goals.

Let's begin our discussion of developing a training plan by exploring the basic ingredients that all triathlon coaches have at their disposal. Planning and strategic oversight of a program are important, and when it comes to designing a training plan, the first step is to determine your ultimate goal for that season. We'll call this your A race. Next, you'll need to determine races of lesser importance you'll use in order to gain competitive experience and develop your race legs. Many elite athletes use these B and C priority events as hard training days to race themselves into shape, both physically and mentally.

Once the race schedule is mapped out and the commitment is made, it's time to start developing your plan, working backward from your A race and using the principle of periodization. Your training ingredients include the variables of intensity, duration, and frequency; the mixture of these components will enable you to develop an effective plan.

For a more nonlinear approach to periodized training, focus on certain energy systems for periods of 4 to 6 weeks, while also incorporating training intensities to bolster other systems simultaneously, because no one energy system is developed at the exclusion of others. For example, an aerobic base development phase will also include some bouts of short, intense work that targets the anaerobic energy system. This makes the transition to a more specific block of hard training much easier while lowering the risk of overtraining and injury.

In addition to cardiorespiratory and sport-specific training, most coaches and athletes now agree that supplemental strength and flexibility training is crucial for enhanced performance and, more important, long-term health and well-being. Supplementary resistance work should be done year-round using a selection of exercises found in this book, with an approach that complements the seasonal training needs of the athlete. For example, when an athlete is in season, the focus of a strength training routine is mostly maintenance and injury prevention. On the other hand, during the preseason, the training focus is more on developing strength and a biomechanically sound foundation.

Table 3.1 shows a sample preseason program used by a beginner to intermediate-level triathlete with one to three years of experience who is preparing for an Olympic-distance triathlon. The emphasis is on aerobic base and basic strength development, with a total training commitment of 10 to 12 hours per week.

From this example, you'll notice that each sport discipline is trained at least three times during the week in addition to three strength training sessions. Athletes should perform sport-specific training before strength work in order to ensure good form and enable solid development of technique. Muscles that are tired because of resistance training can foster poor movement patterns when swimming, cycling, and running, impeding efficiency and wasting energy.

With such a wide variety of strength training exercises from which to choose, it's imperative that you have a focused strategy for continual improvement. Using the expert help of a coach or certified personal trainer, choose from the recommended exercises in this book to create a plan tailored to suit your individual needs.

Table 3.1   Sample Preseason Training Plan for a Beginner to Intermediate Triathlete Training for the Olympic Distance

Day	Triathlon workout routine
Monday	**Rest day:** Focus on recovery after a long weekend of training. Get off your feet as much as possible, eat well, hydrate well, and take good care of yourself. A light massage is recommended.
Tuesday	**Swim workout:** Focus on technique development with plenty of drill work. Don't worry about going fast or hard. Practice good form. Warm-up: 200 to 300 yd or m 8 × 50 drill (catch-up) with 10 sec rest 5 × 100 swim (form focus, reach and glide) with 20 sec rest 6 × 50 drill (fingertip drag) with 10 sec rest 5 × 100 swim (form focus, reach and glide) with 15 sec rest 4 × 50 drill (25 right arm, 25 left arm) with 10 sec rest Cool-down: 200 yd or m **Run workout:** Run 40 min aerobic or up to 5 mi (8 km). Steady-state, aerobic-paced effort (zone 2).
Wednesday	**Brick workout:** Practice a smooth transition from the bike to the run. Bike 1 hr aerobic (zone 2 or 3) at 90 to 100 rpm, then transition to the run for 30 min or up to 3 mi (5 km) at a steady-state aerobic effort. **Strength training:** Full-body circuit workout routine. Move from one exercise to the next in the following sequence, performing 3 rounds: Warm-up: 3 to 5 min light cardio such as jump rope or jumping jacks Push-up (page 56): Perform as many repetitions as possible in 20 to 30 sec Walking lunge (page 131): Take 10 steps with each leg; use hand weights if necessary Stability ball crunch with trunk rotation: Perform for 30 sec Pull-up (page 106) or lat pull-down (page 102): Perform for 20 to 30 sec, or complete up to 15 repetitions

Thursday	**Swim workout:** Warm-up: 200 yd or m 12 × 25 drill (25 right arm, 25 left arm) with 5 sec rest 300 continuous drill (25 kick/scull, 25 form swim, 25 kick/scull, 25 form swim) 8 × 50 drill (alternate catch-up for 50 and fingertip drag for 50) with 15 sec rest 500 pull (steady, swim with good form, aim for distance per stroke) Cool-down: 200 yd or m **Bike workout:** 1 hr aerobic bike with 3 × 5 min tempo with 3 min rest Warm-up: 10 to 15 min at 90 to 100 rpm 3 × 5 min zone 3 or 4 reps (LTHR), 80 to 90 rpm, with 3 min rest and recovery Cool-down: 10 to 15 min
Friday	**Run workout:** Run 40 to 50 min or up to 5 mi (8 km) in aerobic zone 2 **Strength training:** Full-body circuit workout routine. Move from one exercise to the next in the following sequence, performing 3 rounds: Warm-up: 3 to 5 min light cardio such as jump rope or jumping jacks Push-up (page 56): Perform as many repetitions as possible in 20 to 30 sec Walking lunge (page 131): Take 10 steps with each leg; use hand weights if necessary Stability ball crunch with trunk rotation: Perform for 30 sec Pull-up (page 106) or lat pull-down (page 102): Perform for 20 to 30 sec, or complete up to 15 repetitions
Saturday	**Swim workout:** Endurance swim Warm-up: 200 yd or m 6 × 50 drill (choice) with 10 sec rest 2 × 800 steady swim (focus on good form, reach and glide) with 1 min rest Cool-down: 200 yd or m **Bike workout:** 2 hr aerobic endurance ride (zone 2 or 3) at 85 to 95 rpm, steady state
Sunday	**Run workout:** 75 min endurance run (zone 2 or 3) or up to 8 mi (13 km), steady state **Strength training:** Full-body circuit workout routine. Move from one exercise to the next in the following sequence, performing 3 rounds: Warm-up: 3 to 5 min light cardio such as jump rope or jumping jacks Push-up (page 56): Perform as many repetitions as possible in 20 to 30 sec Walking lunge (page 131): Take 10 steps with each leg; use hand weights if necessary Stability ball crunch with trunk rotation: Perform for 30 sec Pull-up (page 106) or lat pull-down (page 102): Perform for 20 to 30 sec, or complete up to 15 repetitions

ARMS

The three disciplines of triathlon—swim, bike, and run—require a balanced use of both lower and upper extremities. The upper extremity is composed of the upper arm, including the humerus; the lower arm, or forearm; the hand; and all muscular attachments. The shoulder, which plays an integral role in upper-extremity function, is discussed in chapter 5.

The arm is suspended from the shoulder by a single bony attachment to the axial skeleton, or trunk, through the clavicle to the chest and sternum. This lack of bony support explains the freedom of motion the arm and shoulder have compared with the lower extremities. Through the coordinated actions of the muscles and the structural support of the ligaments, a triathlete can create a strong anchor to generate propulsion while swimming, maintain strong upper-body support for better aerodynamic positioning on the bike, and help counterbalance the lower-extremity motion during running, creating a smooth and efficient running form.

Weaknesses of any muscles of the arm and forearm may not significantly affect running or biking but can cause significant alterations in swim technique that can lead to injury. Sport-specific strength training can help reduce the chance of repetitive overuse injuries.

The anatomy of the arm can be divided into bones, joints, and muscles.

Bones of the Arm

The humerus is the long bone of the upper arm that links the shoulder to the elbow. It gives shape to the arm and is the attachment site for major muscle groups that provide upper-extremity motion and function.

The forearm consists of two bones: the radius and the ulna. The complex architecture at the ends of each bone and the bow shape of the radius allow complementary motion patterns at the elbow and wrist, including flexion and extension (bending and straightening) and supination and pronation (rotating the hand palm up and palm down). Without these motions, swimming would be impossible.

The wrist and hand are made up of numerous bones that have complex interactions through joints, ligaments, muscles, and their tendon attachments to allow dexterity and a high level of hand function.

Joints of the Arm

The upper extremity has two major joints: the glenohumeral and the elbow. The top portion of the humerus looks like a rounded ball. It sits on the glenoid, or socket, of the scapula. This makes up the bony anatomy of the shoulder. Like all synovial joints, the two ends of the bone are covered with articular cartilage that allows smooth, low-friction motion. They then are covered by a capsule with an inner lining of synovium that produces synovial fluid, which lubricates and nourishes the joint cartilage. This unconstrained joint, like a golf ball sitting on a tee, allows the arm to have significant mobility and range of motion.

The bony architecture of the elbow joint is made up of the distal (far) end of the humerus and the proximal (near) portion of the ulna and radius. Each forearm bone makes a simple hinge joint with the humerus. The humeroulnar articulation allows for flexion and extension, and the humeroradial joint allows for forearm supination and pronation. These simple motions coupled with the articulation between the radius and ulna allow a complex range of motion around the elbow.

Muscles of the Arm

As discussed in chapter 5, a group of muscles in the shoulder, including the rotator cuff, initiate and control shoulder motion. With respect to the upper arm, the pectoralis major and latissimus dorsi insert at the upper end below the level of the rotator cuff on the front of the humerus. When the muscles act independently, they perform primarily arm flexion and extension, respectively. When the muscles act together, they are very powerful adductors and internal rotators of the arm. These motions are essential in the catch and pull phase of swimming.

The biceps brachii takes its origin from two areas of the scapula, the long head at the top of the glenoid and the short head from the coracoid process. These heads join in the middle of the arm along with the brachialis, which originates from the middle to upper end of the humerus, and the brachioradialis, from the distal end of the humerus (figure 4.1). These muscles cross the elbow and perform the motions of both elbow flexion and forearm supination.

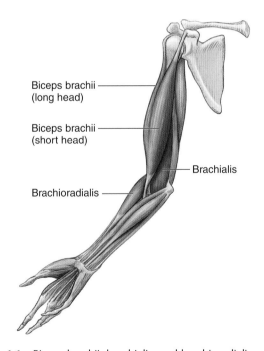

Figure 4.1 Biceps brachii, brachialis, and brachioradialis muscles.

The posterior aspect of the humerus is the origin of the medial and lateral heads of the triceps brachii muscle (figure 4.2). The triceps tendon inserts into the tip of the ulna, or olecranon process. The simple hinge joint of the humeroulnar articulation allows the triceps to extend and straighten the elbow.

Another muscle worth mentioning is the pronator teres. This important muscle arises from the medial aspect of the distal humerus and ulna to allow pronation of the forearm and balance the biceps during forearm supination.

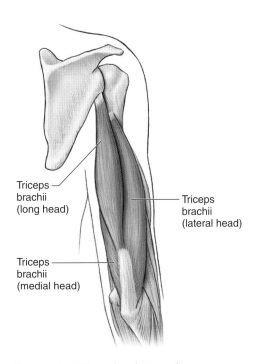

Triceps brachii (long head)

Triceps brachii (lateral head)

Triceps brachii (medial head)

Figure 4.2   Triceps brachii muscle.

The muscles of the forearm (figure 4.3) and hand represent a complex area of anatomy and function. Many activities in life as well as in triathlon—from the swim catch, bike handling, and relaxed proper running form—rely on strong, conditioned forearm musculature.

The forearm can be divided into the flexor group of muscles on the palm side and the extensors on the opposite, or dorsal, surface. The extensor group includes the extensor carpi radialis longus, extensor carpi radialis brevis, and extensor carpi ulnaris of the wrist and the extensor digitorum, extensor digiti minimi, extensor indicis, extensor pollicis longus, and extensor pollicis brevis of the fingers. This group of muscles originates from the outside of the distal humerus, called the lateral epicondyle.

On the palm side of the forearm is the flexor group, which includes the flexor carpi radialis, palmaris longus, and flexor carpi ulnaris of the wrist and the flexor digitorum superficialis, flexor digitorum profundus, and flexor pollicis longus of the fingers. This group of muscles originates from the inside prominence of the medial distal humerus, called the medial epicondyle.

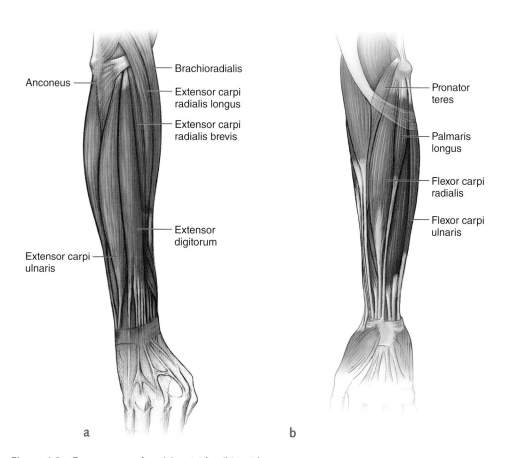

Figure 4.3   Forearm muscles: (a) outside; (b) inside.

Exercises for the Arms

The arm exercises in this chapter build strength and endurance while reducing the risk of injury specific to swimming, cycling, and running. Of course, many other arm exercises are available; it's up to the athlete or coach to select the options appropriate for the athlete's needs.

As when training any body part, begin by performing a sufficient warm-up. A series of dynamic stretches and the use of light resistance are recommended before jumping into your training routine. For example, it is common to see swimmers on deck performing various arm swings as a way to stretch as well as using tubing or light dumbbells in triceps extensions and biceps curling movements to warm up before training.

Training the arms for triathlon performance is similar to training other body parts in that the set and repetition scheme should be geared to developing strength and endurance and not build too much unnecessary mass. (Remember, cycling and running are both affected by the athlete's power-to-weight ratio.) Therefore, we recommend two or three sets of 10 to 15 repetitions for most of the exercises in this chapter.

Triathletes should consider the following when strength training, especially when working the arms. Since recovery is so important when training for three sports, as in triathlon, overdoing any single component can have a negative effect on other areas. When you strength train other upper-body parts, such as the chest, shoulders, and upper back, the arms are used as well and receive a training effect. Be careful not to overtrain the arms by adding too many arm-specific exercises to your routine. Keep an eye on the gauges or work with a coach to make sure you're following the proper training program.

Close-Grip Push-Up

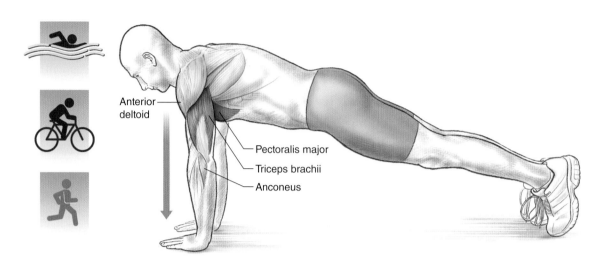

Anterior deltoid

Pectoralis major

Triceps brachii

Anconeus

Execution

1. Lying facedown, place your hands slightly narrower than shoulder-width apart, with your fingers pointing forward.
2. Extend your body so that your spine is straight. Support your lower body on your toes, with straight and locked legs. Keep your head in a neutral position, aligned with your spine.
3. Lower your body slowly and under control until your chest is 1 to 2 inches (2.5 to 5 cm) from the ground. Keep your upper arms close to your body.
4. Press up slowly and under control, maintaining a straight body position, until your elbows are almost locked. Repeat for the desired number of repetitions.

Muscles Involved

Primary: Triceps brachii, pectoralis major

Secondary: Pectoralis minor, anterior deltoid, anconeus

Triathlon Focus

The push-up is considered the king of upper-body strengthening exercises. Push-ups are easy to perform, don't require any equipment, and are very effective at producing results, enhancing both strength and endurance in the upper-body musculature.

By varying the hand position of the push-up movement, the athlete can focus on activating slightly different muscle groups. In this example of the close-grip push-up, the emphasis is on the triceps brachii, a muscle used extensively in swimming and cycling. In the freestyle swim stroke, much of the athlete's forward propulsion is created in the final extension phase of the stroke. Here, a strong triceps will be able to propel the hand through the water with more force, resulting in a faster swim pace.

Building arm strength can help with safer riding by enhancing bike handling and stability. Cycling hand positions vary according to the terrain and objectives. Strong triceps assist the rider in supporting her body weight when riding on the hoods or the drops and when riding out of the saddle and help stabilize the upper body more when riding on the aerobars.

VARIATION

Push-Up From Knee Position

Close-grip push-ups isolate the triceps, making this exercise difficult for some people. One variation that makes this exercise easier for beginners is to perform the movement from the knees. Be sure to keep the same body position, with a straight spine and a neutral head position. Once you can perform the desired number of repetitions from the knees, gradually move to performing reps from your toes.

Bent-Over Freestyle Pull With Band

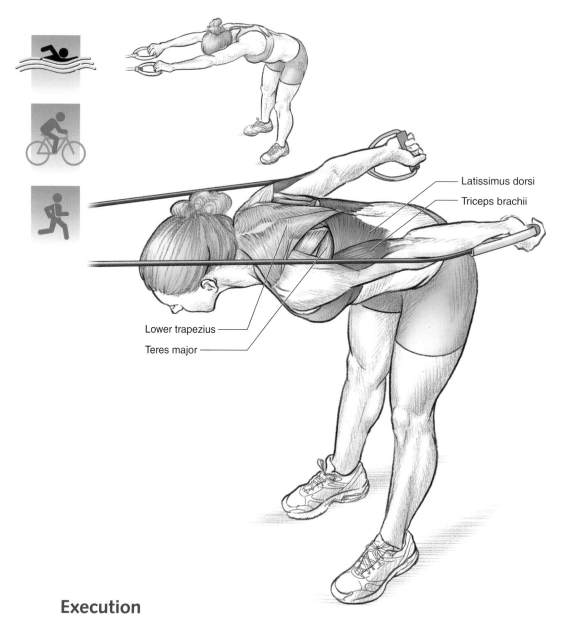

Latissimus dorsi

Triceps brachii

Lower trapezius

Teres major

Execution

1. Choose a band resistance suitable for your current fitness level. Anchor the band to an immovable object such as a piece of weight equipment or a doorjamb. The band should be near waist height. Grasp the handles or the ends of the band with your palms facing behind you.

2. Step back from the anchor in order to create some tension in the band. Stand with your feet shoulder-width apart and knees slightly bent.

3. Bend over at the waist so your upper body is almost parallel to the ground. Stretch your arms above your head, as if you were entering the water in the first phase of the freestyle swim stroke.

4. Using both arms simultaneously, pull back on the handles with your elbows slightly up (high elbows) and bent, activating the chest and upper-back muscles.

5. When the hands reach the waist, extend the forearms back against the increasing resistance of the stretched band, focusing on the triceps and almost locking the elbows in a fully extended position.

6. Return in a controlled manner against the resistance of the elastic band and repeat. Complete three to five sets of 10 to 15 repetitions.

Muscles Involved

Primary: Latissimus dorsi, pectoralis major, triceps brachii

Secondary: Lower trapezius, teres major

Triathlon Focus

This is a key dryland exercise used by swimmers. Convenient and specific to the freestyle swim movement, the bent-over freestyle pull with band should be a staple exercise for the busy triathlete who is challenged to find enough time to get to the pool as well as for the triathlete who wishes to supplement his swim training with band work.

The key muscles engaged in this movement include those of the upper back and chest as well as the triceps in the arms. The ability to mimic the movement pattern found in an effective freestyle swim technique—including an early vertical forearm, high elbow, and explosive final extension of the triceps—against the increasing resistance of the band helps enhance swim efficiency while also boosting swim-specific strength and endurance.

VARIATION

Single-Arm Pull

Instead of pulling with both arms at the same time, a simple variation is to pull with one arm at a time. Focusing on one arm allows you to practice your swim cadence with proper body rotation.

Dumbbell Kickback

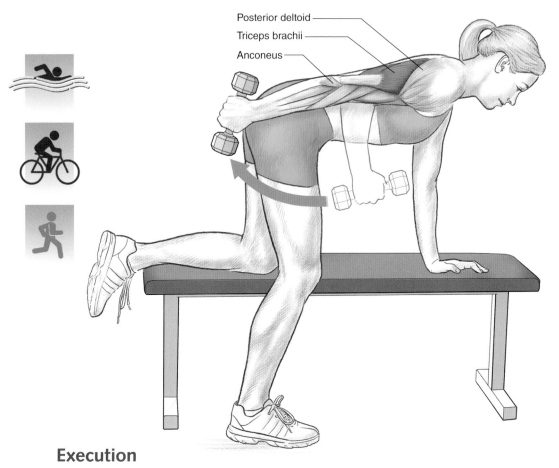

Posterior deltoid
Triceps brachii
Anconeus

Execution

1. Lean on a weight bench with your left knee and left arm supporting your weight. Hold a dumbbell in your right hand.

2. With your back straight and your head in a neutral position, hold your upper arm along your side so it's aligned with your upper body, parallel to the floor.

3. Keeping your upper arm stationary at the shoulder, lower the dumbbell to a 90-degree bent-elbow position so that the forearm is perpendicular to the floor. This is the starting position.

4. Raise the dumbbell on a steady count of one and two and three, focusing on engaging the triceps brachii, back to the straight-arm position until the elbow is almost locked. Return to the starting position, again at a steady and controlled rate of speed.

5. Repeat for the required number of repetitions with your right arm, and then switch sides and perform the exercise with the left arm.

Muscles Involved

Primary: Triceps brachii

Secondary: Posterior deltoid, latissimus dorsi, anconeus

Triathlon Focus

The triceps are key muscles used constantly by both cyclists and swimmers. The cyclist needs strong triceps with highly developed endurance characteristics in order to support her upper-body weight when seated or standing, especially during rides of 2 hours or more. The swimmer needs strong and explosive triceps to aid in efficiently propelling him through the water during the final phase of the stroke, especially when using the freestyle stroke. Although just swimming and cycling will develop the triceps, adding resistance training such as the dumbbell kickback will take that development to the next level, further enhancing performance.

An emphasis on good form is important with this exercise in particular; some athletes tend to throw the weight back as opposed to using the triceps to generate the force. Therefore it's important to perform the exercise slowly, counting to two or three on each phase (concentric and eccentric) of the movement, avoiding a pendulum-like swinging motion. Another consideration with regard to proper technique is keeping the spine straight with a neutral head position, helping alleviate the possibility of back strain.

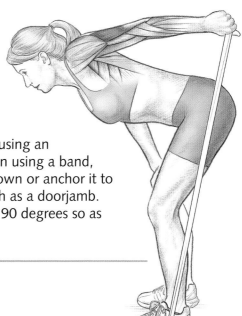

VARIATION

Band Kickback

This movement can be done effectively using an elastic band instead of a dumbbell. When using a band, either anchor it beneath your foot as shown or anchor it to an immovable object in front of you such as a doorjamb. Keep the elbow joint angle greater than 90 degrees so as not to overstress the joint.

Dumbbell Curl

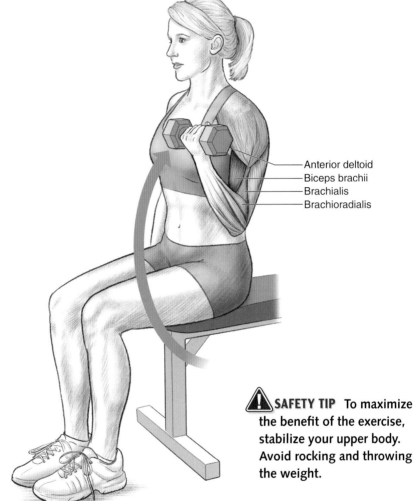

Anterior deltoid
Biceps brachii
Brachialis
Brachioradialis

⚠️ **SAFETY TIP** To maximize the benefit of the exercise, stabilize your upper body. Avoid rocking and throwing the weight.

Execution

1. Stand erect or sit on a weight bench as shown. Grab dumbbells of an appropriate weight for your fitness level, one dumbbell in each hand. Lower your arms to your sides, palms turned in.

2. With your left arm, curl the weight slowly toward the shoulder, rotating the wrist so the palm is facing the shoulder.

3. Lower the dumbbell to the extended position, and repeat with the right arm for the required number of repetitions.

Muscles Involved

Primary: Biceps brachii

Secondary: Brachialis, brachioradialis, anterior deltoid, forearm flexors

Triathlon Focus

Triathletes require strong biceps in order to stabilize their position on the bike, swim with greater efficiency, and drive with their arms when running uphill or sprinting to the finish.

Having strong biceps is of particular importance during the bike leg and time trials. When riding in the aero position, triathletes engage the biceps by pulling up hard on the bars, using the bars as an anchor for leverage and stabilization.

For the runner, especially the long-distance triathlete participating in half-Ironman and Ironman races, strong biceps with enhanced endurance will aid in achieving faster run times by enabling the athlete to maintain proper running form and biomechanics.

VARIATION

Stability Ball Dumbbell Curl

One popular variation is to perform the curl while seated on a stability ball. This engages the core muscle groups in addition to the biceps.

Wrist Curl

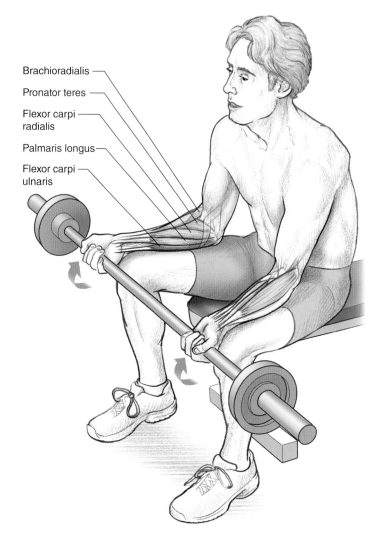

Brachioradialis

Pronator teres

Flexor carpi radialis

Palmaris longus

Flexor carpi ulnaris

Execution

1. Sit on a weight bench with a barbell or dumbbells in your hands. Place the backs of your forearms on your thighs, with your wrists hanging over the knees and the palms facing up.
2. Gently lower the weight at the wrists, engaging the forearm muscles.
3. Raise the weight by flexing the wrists toward the ceiling as high as possible. Repeat this movement for the required number of repetitions.

Muscles Involved

Primary: Flexor carpi ulnaris

Secondary: Brachioradialis, pronator teres, flexor carpi radialis, palmaris longus

Triathlon Focus

Conditioning the forearms and building overall grip strength are often overlooked by triathletes but are very important.

For cycling, grip strength allows the rider to grab the base-bar extensions for more secure and aggressive climbing, as well as the aerobar extensions for enhanced stability and balance when time trialing.

The swimmer requires strong forearms to maintain proper hand position with extended fingers throughout the stroke and to avoid fatigue.

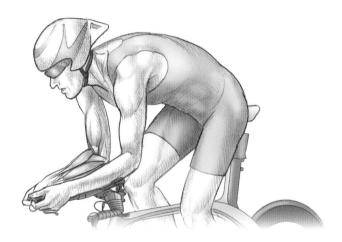

VARIATION

Wrist Roller

A wrist roller can be used to improve forearm strength. Perform the exercise with the palms facing up toward the ceiling while rolling the weight with a spindle.

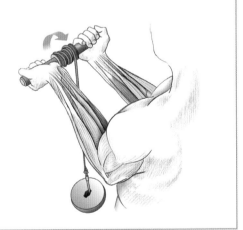

SHOULDERS

The complex anatomy of the shoulder makes it one of the largest and most functional joints in the body. The shoulder, which is made up of three bones (the humerus, scapula, and clavicle) along with numerous muscles, tendons, and ligaments, positions the arm in space, creating structural support and generating power for all athletic activities.

Eighteen separate muscles either arise from or insert into the scapula, or shoulder blade. The muscle coordination involved in arm elevation and activities such as swimming, biking, running, and training is as involved as any complex machine. The muscles create shoulder motion that takes place at two distinct joints. The glenohumeral joint is formed between the top of the arm bone and the scapula, and the scapulothoracic joint is formed by the scapula as it sits on the back of the chest, or thoracic, area. If one segment breaks down, the rest of the system has to compensate for the injured part, which could cause pain and dysfunction. The repetitive nature of triathlon sports, most notably swimming, makes the shoulder a prime area for potential overuse and injury. A complete understanding of the interactions between the anatomical structures and of the benefits of strength training can help an athlete train safely and prevent injuries.

Bony Anatomy of the Shoulder

The shoulder is made up of three bones: the scapula, clavicle, and humerus (figure 5.1). The humerus, as discussed in chapter 4, is a long bone with an upper end shaped like a ball that makes an articulation, or joint, with the shallow socket of the scapula (the glenoid). It is like a golf ball sitting on a tee. This configuration allows for tremendous mobility of the shoulder.

The scapula, or shoulder blade, which sits on the posterior chest wall, is triangular in shape. The acromion is a bony projection from the scapula that forms its top border. It can easily be felt as the bony prominence on top of the shoulder. It functions as a bony arch to protect the rotator cuff muscles and tendons that run below it.

The clavicle, or collarbone, is a long bone that lies horizontally across the front of the chest. Via the acromioclavicular joint, the clavicle attaches the scapula to the

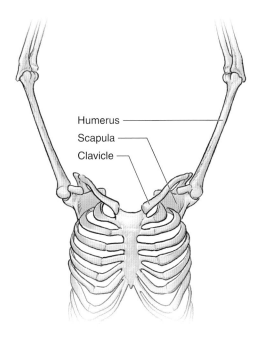

Figure 5.1 Bones of the shoulder: scapula, clavicle, and humerus.

sternum, or breastbone. The clavicle functions as the sole bony attachment and mechanical strut from which the shoulder and arm are suspended. It helps keep the arm supported away from the body to allow maximum range of motion.

Ligaments of the Shoulder

The golf ball and tee analogy of the shoulder joint, or glenohumeral articulation, helps us understand how mobile the shoulder can be, but this potentially unstable configuration means the ball can fall off the tee. Medically it is called a dislocation when the ball falls off and a subluxation when it starts to roll off but rolls back into place. Often acute trauma such as a fall from the bike can cause a dislocation, but repetitive injury from swimming may lead to subluxations, which may be recurrent or chronic. Muscle coordination about the shoulder, a soft-tissue envelope around the joint, and an intact ligament system prevent this from happening.

A tough fibrous-tissue capsule surrounds the shoulder joint, like a balloon with the air sucked out, holding the ball on the tee. Thickenings of this tissue form a ligament system, connecting bone to bone, that also provides stability. These ligaments attach to a ring of tissue called the labrum that surrounds the glenoid. It helps deepen the socket and provide further resistance to the ball's falling off the tee.

Muscles of the Shoulder

The muscles of the shoulder girdle can be divided into three groups: major movers, fine-tune coordinators, and scapular stabilizers. Six primary movements are created by the coordinated actions of muscles from each group working together:

> **Flexion:** arm elevation in front of the body
>
> **Extension:** arm motion behind the body
>
> **Abduction:** arm elevation away from the body (to the side)
>
> **Adduction:** arm movement toward the body (from the side)
>
> **Internal rotation:** rotation of the arm toward and across the body
>
> **External rotation:** rotation of the arm away from the body

Major Movers

The major movers include the deltoid, latissimus dorsi, and pectoralis major.

The deltoid (figure 5.2) is made up of three distinct heads. The anterior, middle, and posterior heads originate at the clavicle, acromion, and spine of the scapula and insert as a single tendon onto the upper end of the humerus. When all fibers contract simultaneously, the deltoid is the prime mover for abduction.

The latissimus dorsi (figure 5.3) is the broad muscle of the back. It originates at the lower back and rib region, runs under the armpit, or axilla, and inserts on the medial, or inside, aspect of the proximal humerus. It acts as a shoulder extensor and adductor. It also serves as an internal rotator in conjunction with the pectoralis. Swim propulsion depends on technique and the strength of this muscle.

The pectoralis major and smaller pectoralis minor are fan-shaped muscles that lie on the anterior chest, arising from the clavicle, sternum, and upper ribs. They attach to the medial part of the upper end of the humerus. Their primary actions include arm flexion, adduction, and internal rotation. The strength of the pectoralis is a factor in swimming speed. The pectoralis major and pectoralis minor are covered in more detail in chapter 6.

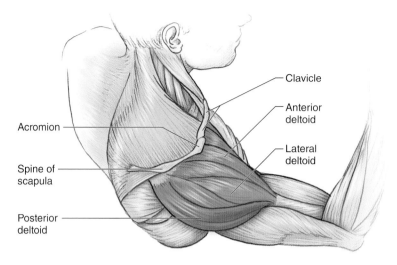

Figure 5.2   Deltoid muscle.

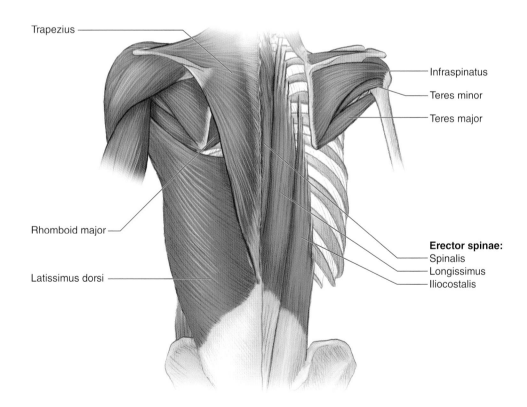

Figure 5.3   Back muscles, including the latissimus dorsi.

Fine-Tune Coordinators

The fine-tune coordinators make up the rotator cuff (figure 5.4). The rotator cuff is a group of four small muscles (the subscapularis, supraspinatus, infraspinatus, and teres minor) that originate from the scapula and together form a tendinous cuff that surrounds the head of the humerus. The subscapularis functions as an internal rotator of the shoulder. The supraspinatus, as it lies on top of the scapula, helps with abduction. The infraspinatus and teres minor assist with external rotation.

As the deltoid begins to move the arm, the rotator cuff muscles contract in a coordinated fashion to compress the humeral head onto the glenoid, thus holding the ball on the tee. Repetitive activities or trauma from a fall may injure the cuff tendons, leading to a spectrum of conditions, including impingement syndrome, bursitis, rotator cuff tendinitis, and rotator cuff tears, that cause pain and disability.

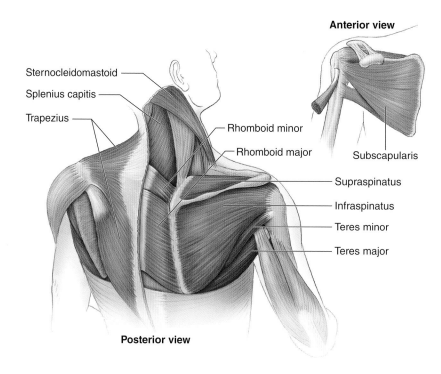

Figure 5.4 Rotator cuff and scapula muscles.

Scapular Stabilizers

This group of muscles includes the trapezius, rhomboid major, rhomboid minor, serratus anterior, levator scapulae, and pectoralis minor. These muscles are responsible for scapular movement. As the humerus moves, the scapula follows with the motions of elevation, depression, retraction, and protraction. The combination of scapular motion on the posterior rib cage and motion at the shoulder joint is what allows us to put our arms in such a wide variety of positions.

For shoulder motion to occur, the different pieces of the complex shoulder anatomy must coordinate. This highlights the importance of having a strong and well-conditioned shoulder joint. The exercises that follow emphasize these muscle groups.

Exercises for the Shoulder

The shoulder complex is relatively delicate and requires special care and deliberation when training. Place special focus on performing movements with good technique. Heavy weights and low repetitions are not ideally suited for most endurance athletes. Typically the ideal target is three or four sets of 10 to 15 repetitions, with 60 to 90 seconds of rest between each set. The weight chosen for each set should be challenging yet not impossible. You should be able to complete the targeted number of repetitions. As always, a proper warm-up of the shoulder is suggested before initiating any resistance training routine.

Forward Dumbbell Deltoid Raise

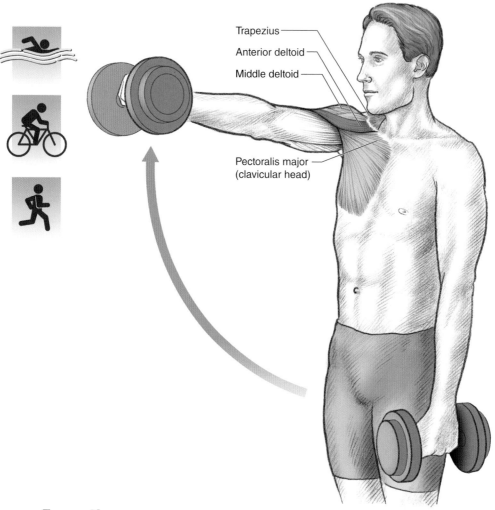

Trapezius

Anterior deltoid

Middle deltoid

Pectoralis major
(clavicular head)

Execution

1. Stand holding a dumbbell in each hand, with your arms hanging at your sides. Your palms should be facing your thighs, arms relaxed.
2. Keep your back straight, and focus on engaging your core as you slowly raise one dumbbell directly in front of your body.
3. As the dumbbell rises, slightly bend your elbow and rotate your hand so your palm faces the floor at the top of the movement.
4. Lower the dumbbell slowly and under control as you begin the movement with the opposite arm.

Muscles Involved

Primary: Anterior deltoid

Secondary: Pectoralis major, middle deltoid, trapezius

Triathlon Focus

The anterior deltoid plays an important role in swimming, cycling, and running. In swimming, the anterior deltoid is indirectly engaged in the catch and in the first part of the pulling phase of the freestyle stroke. Cyclists use this muscle group to assist in stabilizing their position when standing to climb while grasping the base bars. Runners leverage the front of the shoulder when driving with the arms to aid in climbing steep hills.

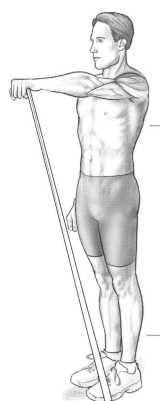

Forward Deltoid Raise With Tubing

Stretch tubes are ideal for triathletes because of their convenience and ease of application in performing a variety of upper-body movements, including the forward deltoid raise. Vary the resistance according to your needs by choosing the correct tube weight or by varying your distance from the anchor, which can be your foot as illustrated or any stationary object.

Lateral Dumbbell Deltoid Raise

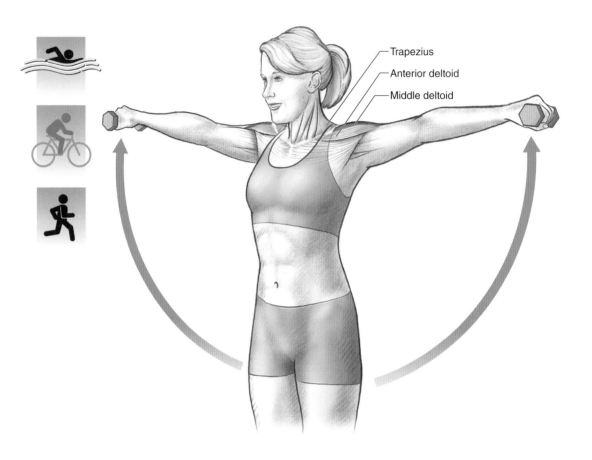

Trapezius

Anterior deltoid

Middle deltoid

Execution

1. Stand holding a dumbbell in each hand down at your sides, with your palms facing your thighs.
2. Slightly bending your arms at the elbows, raise your arms laterally in a slow and controlled motion until they are even with your shoulders. Keep your palms facing the ground.
3. Lower the dumbbells to the starting position, and repeat for the required number of repetitions.

Muscles Involved

Primary: Middle deltoid

Secondary: Anterior deltoid, posterior deltoid, supraspinatus, trapezius

Triathlon Focus

The middle deltoid, like the anterior deltoid, plays more of a supporting role than a primary role for all shoulder movement patterns involved in swimming freestyle, cycling, and running.

The swimmer heavily relies on this muscle group during the recovery phase of the freestyle stroke. Premature fatigue of this muscle group when swimming open-water distance freestyle, especially when swimming heads up to sight buoys and to navigate the course, can cause asymmetry in the stroke. This sloppiness can slow a swimmer's time. Additionally, long-sleeved wetsuits tend to be tight around the shoulder, creating even more fatigue and the need for stronger middle deltoids.

During running, good posture and arm swing are necessary to maintain proper form, especially when fatigue starts to settle in. Focus on developing the middle deltoid to strengthen form overall.

Dumbbell Shoulder Press

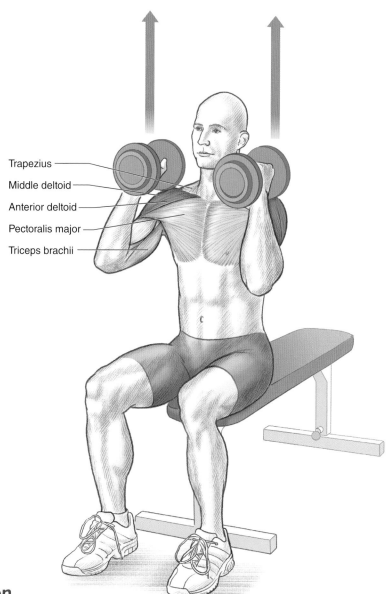

Trapezius

Middle deltoid

Anterior deltoid

Pectoralis major

Triceps brachii

Execution

1. Sit on a bench with your back straight. Hold two dumbbells of the same weight on your shoulders, palms facing your body.
2. Press the dumbbells straight overhead until your elbows are almost locked out. Rotating the palms during this movement may help prevent impingement of the biceps tendon.
3. Lower the dumbbells slowly back to the starting position, and repeat for the required number of repetitions.

Muscles Involved

Primary: Anterior deltoid, middle deltoid

Secondary: Pectoralis major, posterior deltoid, trapezius, supraspinatus, triceps brachii

Triathlon Focus

People are weakest when it comes to overhead resistance exercises. The dumbbell shoulder press is an effective exercise that engages several important muscle groups at the same time, including the middle deltoid, anterior deltoid, and triceps brachii.

For the swimmer, this exercise will help the athlete extend and reach, a component in creating a streamlined body position and maximizing strokes per length.

The cyclist will benefit from this movement by building overall shoulder as well as trapezius and upper-arm strength. This is especially important for the long-distance triathlete who spends a lot of time with his arms rested in the aero position and with his neck bent slightly, looking up the road.

VARIATION

Stability Ball Shoulder Press

This movement can also function as a core strengthening and balance exercise. Simply by performing the presses using a stability ball instead of a bench, you'll be able to gain those important benefits.

Internal Rotation With Tubing

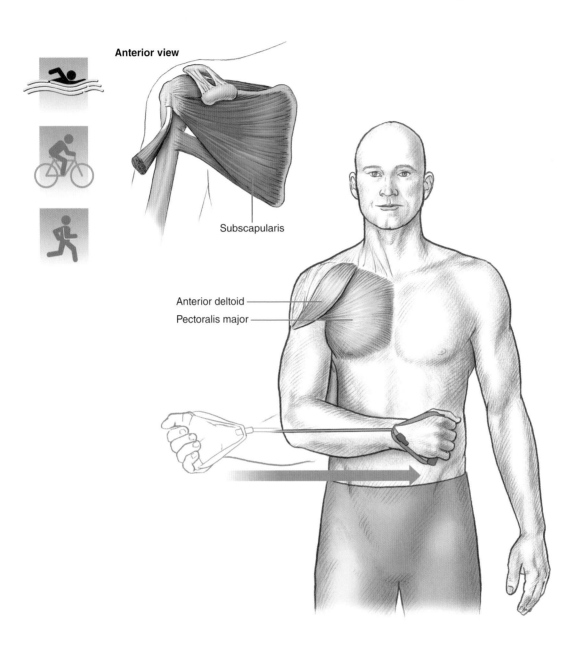

Anterior view

Subscapularis

Anterior deltoid

Pectoralis major

Execution

1. Choose exercise tubing of an appropriate resistance for your fitness level. Secure the tubing to an anchor at elbow height, and stand approximately 4 feet (1.2 m) away from the anchor. Hold the handle with the arm closest to the anchor, and bend the elbow 90 degrees. Place a small, folded towel between the elbow and chest. Holding the elbow in this position will reinforce proper rotation technique.

2. Keeping the forearm parallel to the floor and the upper arm stable, rotate your hand across the front of your body until your hand touches your torso.

3. Return slowly to the starting position, and repeat for the required number of repetitions.

Muscles Involved

Primary: Subscapularis

Secondary: Pectoralis major, anterior deltoid, latissimus dorsi

Triathlon Focus

This exercise is included in this section because of its importance in maintaining rotator cuff health, with the goal of preventing shoulder-related overuse injuries often encountered by masters swimmers and triathletes. As one of four rotator cuff muscles, the subscapularis is the muscle responsible for internal rotation of the arm. Together with the shoulder capsule and ligament system, the subscapularis acts as a shoulder stabilizer, helping to keep the ball on the tee. Although other larger muscles perform similar actions of internal rotation, the subscapularis should be targeted with supplemental strength training in order to reduce the risks associated with repetitive motion movements such as swimming freestyle for distance events.

External Rotation With Tubing

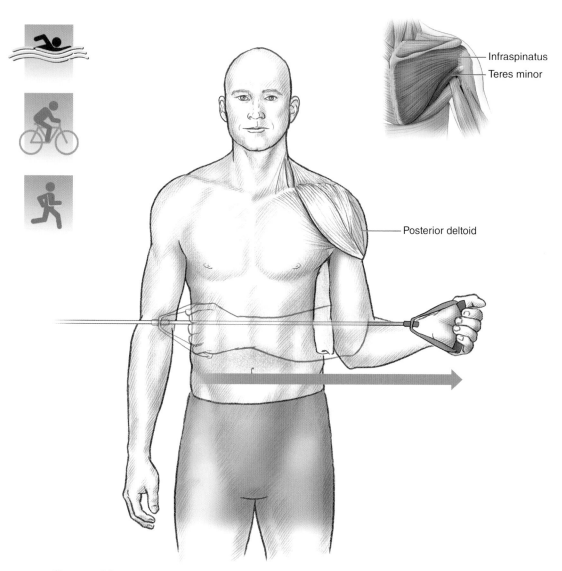

Infraspinatus

Teres minor

Posterior deltoid

Execution

1. With exercise tubing of the appropriate resistance, stand approximately 4 feet (1.2 m) away from an anchor for the tube, set at elbow height. Bend the arm at 90 degrees, holding the tube with the arm farthest from the anchor. Place a small, folded towel between the elbow and chest. Holding the elbow in this position will reinforce proper rotation technique.

2. Keeping the forearm parallel to the floor and the upper arm stable, rotate your hand across and away from the front of your body.

3. Return slowly to the side, and repeat for the required number of repetitions.

Muscles Involved

Primary: Infraspinatus, teres minor

Secondary: Posterior deltoid

Triathlon Focus

Similar to the internal rotation with tubing exercise, this exercise is included in this section because of its importance in preventing shoulder-related overuse injuries often encountered by masters swimmers and triathletes. External rotation of the arm is an essential movement pattern in swimming. Fatigue of this group of muscles can cause dyskinesia (abnormal motion about the shoulder and scapula), which leads to injury. These strength training exercises increase the durability of this group of muscles, which in turn helps reduce the chance of injury.

Upright Row

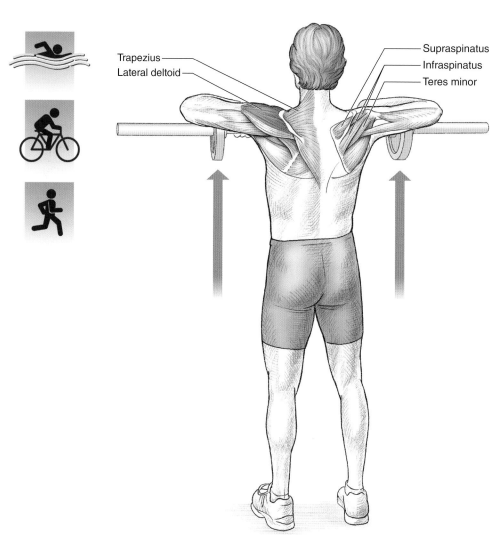

Trapezius

Lateral deltoid

Supraspinatus

Infraspinatus

Teres minor

Execution

1. Stand holding a barbell in front of you, resting the barbell against your thighs with your arms straight.
2. Pull the weight up vertically along your torso until it reaches your upper chest near the base of your neck. Focus on keeping your elbows high and engaging the various shoulder muscles during the movement.
3. Return to the starting position, and repeat for the required number of repetitions.

Muscles Involved

Primary: Anterior deltoid, lateral deltoid

Secondary: Infraspinatus, supraspinatus, teres minor, trapezius

Triathlon Focus

Each discipline of triathlon relies on strong shoulders, and the upright row is an excellent multijoint exercise that focuses on this area of the body. From the swimmer's perspective, strong shoulders mean stronger pulls through the water and less fatigue during the recovery phase of the stroke when the swimmer is wearing a long-sleeved wetsuit. The cyclist will enjoy having stronger shoulders when rocking the bike back and forth while out of the saddle and climbing. Strong shoulders also prevent fatigue when riding for countless hours on the aerobars. The runner will be able to maintain a strong rhythm and balance, driving with the arms when attacking a climb or sprinting to the finish. The upright row addresses practically all of these important aspects.

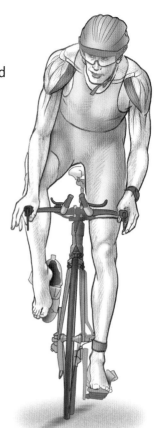

VARIATION

Upright Row With Dumbbells, Cables, or Elastic Bands

The upright rowing movement can be performed effectively using dumbbells, cables, or elastic bands.

Single-Arm Dumbbell Row

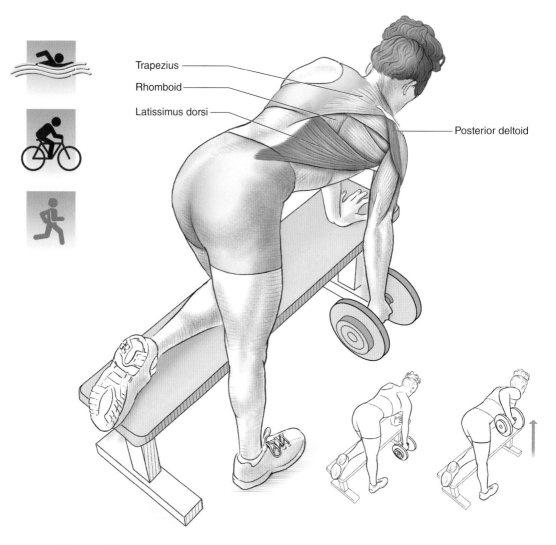

Trapezius

Rhomboid

Latissimus dorsi

Posterior deltoid

Execution

1. Kneel on a bench on one knee. Place your hand on the bench on the same side to support your weight. Bend down to pick up a dumbbell off the floor, and then let the weight hang vertically.
2. Keeping your back flat and your head in a neutral position, bring your hand up until it reaches the side of your lower chest.
3. Return the dumbbell to the starting position, and repeat for the required number of repetitions for that arm. Switch arms and repeat.

Muscles Involved

Primary: Posterior deltoid, latissimus dorsi

Secondary: Trapezius, rhomboid major, rhomboid minor, biceps brachii

Triathlon Focus

The single-arm dumbbell row targets the posterior deltoid, an important muscle to develop for the swimming and cycling legs of triathlon.

Open-water freestyle swimming requires high arm recovery because of rough waters and crowded wave starts. Having a strong rear deltoid lessens fatigue and improves the athlete's stroke cycles in difficult open-water swimming conditions.

Cyclists require strong rear deltoids primarily when grabbing the base bars for hard climbing and sprinting. The single-arm dumbbell row activates many of the same muscle groups involved when aggressively rocking the bike back and forth during hard, out-of-the-saddle efforts.

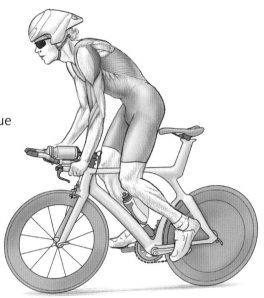

VARIATION

Single-Arm Cable or Elastic Band Pull

Sit on a weight bench as shown or a stability ball. Perform the one-arm rowing motion using a horizontally oriented cable or elastic band. This variation offers the added benefit of core stabilization.

CHAPTER 6

CHEST

No discussion about the upper extremity can be complete without an understanding of how the chest musculature affects the motion and stability of the shoulder. The pectoralis major, pectoralis minor, and serratus anterior as a muscle group make up some of the most visible muscles in the body. From late-night infomercials on how to make the chest muscles bigger, to the muscle-bound bodybuilders on the cover of magazines, the front of the chest has come to represent strength and power.

For the triathlete, size does not matter and is often even feared with weight training. As discussed in the last two chapters, motion of the shoulder is accomplished through the intricate coordination of many muscles. The strength and health of the chest musculature form just another link in the chain to help develop efficiency, improve performance, and prevent injuries about the shoulder.

Bony Structures of the Chest

The bony anatomy of the chest consists of the anterior ribs, sternum, and clavicle. As mentioned in chapter 4, the clavicle is the only bony attachment of the arm and shoulder to the main body. The clavicle is bound to the sternum by the strong sternoclavicular joint. In conjunction with the pectoralis muscle, the clavicle anchors the arm and shoulder to the chest wall. It is through the pectoralis muscle contraction and the mechanical strut action of the clavicle that we are able to push objects away from the chest.

The ribs, as expected, protect internal structures such as the lungs and heart. The intercostal muscles that lie between each rib work with the diaphragm with the assistance of the pectoralis major and serratus anterior muscles to allow us to breathe deeply, as is needed with exercise.

Muscles of the Chest

The pectoralis major (figure 6.1) is a large fan-shaped muscle that has two points of origin. The clavicular head, or upper portion, arises from the medial clavicle and upper portion of the sternum, called the manubrium. The sternal head, or lower portion, originates from the sternum and upper ribs. Muscle fibers from both origins then converge and run laterally outward to form a tendon that attaches to the medial, inner portion of the upper humerus. Although rare, injuries to this tendon occur during high-intensity activities including powerlifting and American football. Unfortunately many of these injuries require surgical intervention to restore anatomy and preserve function. The main actions of the pectoralis major are flexion, adduction, and internal rotation of the arm and shoulder. In swimming the pectoralis major, with the help of the latissimus dorsi, helps initiate the pull. During cycling in the aerobars or on the hoods, the pectoralis major helps support the upper body, and in running it assists in fluid arm motion.

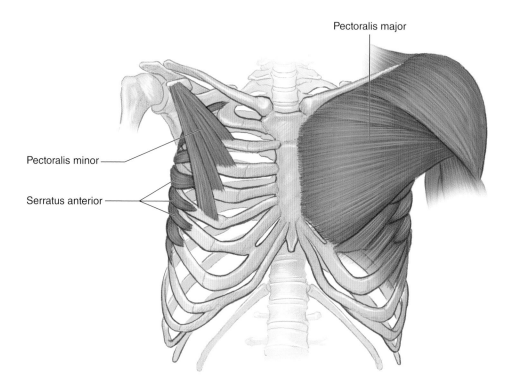

Figure 6.1   Muscles of the chest.

The pectoralis minor, which is a smaller muscle, lies beneath the pectoralis major. It takes its origin from the anterior upper ribs and inserts into the medial border of the scapula and a bony projection from the scapula called the coracoid process. Its function is to help control the scapula, stabilizing it against the thoracic wall during arm elevation.

The serratus anterior, known as the boxer's muscle, is a deep muscle group that originates from the upper ribs on each side of the chest and inserts along the entire length of the medial scapula. Its function, stabilization of the scapula, is similar to that of the pectoralis minor. It helps pull the scapula forward during the recovery and initial catch phases of swimming. During breathing, the serratus anterior also assists in chest expansion.

Exercises for the Chest

Common strength training exercises that many athletes learn early in their careers, including the bench press, military press, and dip, preferentially strengthen the front of the shoulder and chest. If these exercises are done exclusively, this can cause the shoulders to roll forward because of muscle imbalance and subsequently may cause stiffness in the front of the shoulders. In swimming, this contracted position may cause the rotator cuff to overwork, leading to a spectrum of injuries including shoulder impingement. Symptoms commonly include shoulder pain and limited motion. In cycling, weak chest and upper-extremity muscles plus a rounded shoulder position put the neck and upper back at risk for a soft-tissue injury, called a strain. Symptoms of this type of strain may manifest as difficulty staying in the aerobars and even difficulty keeping the head up when riding for extended periods. In running, a rounded shoulder position can cause a constriction of the chest wall, limiting chest expansion and proper breathing, and an abnormal arm motion, such as swinging across the body, that can decrease running efficiency.

The following exercises, which include the simple push-up and dip, need to be balanced with exercises that target scapular rotators, fine-tune coordinators, and the power muscles of the back. Increased emphasis on the less sexy muscles including the back and rotator cuff will pay large dividends with respect to injury prevention. A simple ratio of 2:1 back-to-chest strength training will keep you healthy.

Heavier weights and fewer repetitions yield considerable muscle size and strength gains, while lighter weights and higher repetitions enhance muscular endurance without adding bulk. For the triathlete, the power-to-weight ratio is a key factor in performance, especially in cycling and running, since gravity and wind resistance play a key role in affecting velocity. Therefore building muscular strength and endurance without packing on additional weight is a goal. For most of the exercises in this chapter, perform two or three sets of 10 to 15 repetitions. Select weights that enable you to finish the required number of repetitions but with considerable effort for the last few repetitions. As you become more experienced in strength training, you may choose to perform one or two sets to exhaustion, a point at which another repetition or two would be nearly impossible without assistance from a spotter. This is an advanced training technique that should be used only by experienced athletes during certain phases of their annual training cycling so as to prevent overtraining and reduce the risk of injury.

Push-Up

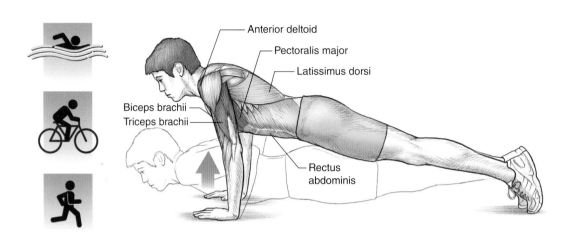

Execution

1. Start in a prone position, with hands slightly wider than shoulder width and fingers pointed forward.
2. With your core engaged, lower your torso until it lightly touches the ground. Maintain a flat back and neutral head position.
3. With an explosive yet controlled motion, press up to the starting position, keeping elbows slightly bent upon completion. Repeat for the required number of repetitions.

Muscles Involved

Primary: Pectoralis major, triceps brachii, anterior deltoid

Secondary: Biceps brachii, latissimus dorsi, rectus abdominis

Triathlon Focus

One of the most effective and popular upper-body exercises available, the push-up targets key muscle groups in the torso and upper arms that are engaged during swimming, cycling, and running. And because it is easy to do and doesn't require any additional equipment, the basic push-up is convenient and can be performed practically anywhere.

Swimmers will benefit by developing stronger chest muscles, especially the pectoralis major, and the triceps brachii muscles essential during execution of the freestyle stroke. Enhanced strength in these muscle groups can result in greater endurance and power to pull the body through the water.

Pure cyclists and runners, with a few exceptions, are notoriously weak in the upper body. However, triathletes tend to be stronger because of the swim leg, and the strength developed by performing push-ups can help the triathlete stabilize himself better on the bike when climbing hills out of the saddle. The runner will benefit by experiencing less upper-body fatigue during hard uphill run intervals and will be able to drive the arms with greater force in case he needs to sprint to the finish line.

VARIATION

Push-Up From the Knees

Many triathletes new to upper-body strength training, and push-ups in particular, will need to modify the push-up by starting from their knees instead of their toes. This makes the exercise easier to perform and enables the weaker athlete to focus on form while developing strength. Once you are able to perform a few sets of 12 to 15 repetitions from the knees, it's time to begin incorporating reps from the toes.

Dumbbell Stability Ball Chest Press

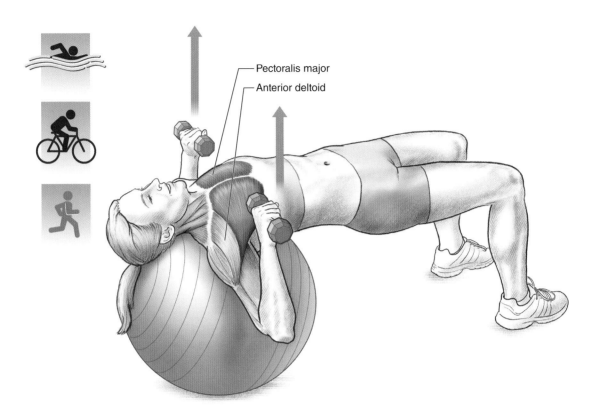

Pectoralis major
Anterior deltoid

Execution

1. Sitting on a stability ball with a dumbbell of appropriate weight in each hand, slide your back down onto the ball until your upper back is firmly in place and you feel stable.

2. With your legs slightly wider than shoulder width for increased stability, your hips straight in line with your shoulders and head, and your arms extended, slowly lower the dumbbells to chest level.

3. Press up, returning to the starting position while being careful to maintain balance on the unstable surface of the ball.

Muscles Involved

Primary: Pectoralis major

Secondary: Anterior deltoid, triceps brachii

Triathlon Focus

This movement offers many of the same benefits as other pressing exercises, engaging and strengthening the muscles of the chest, anterior shoulder, and triceps. By using a stability ball, this variation offers the additional benefits of developing a sense of balance and strengthening the core.

Because this exercise requires weight stabilization and balance with each individual arm (user dependent), it benefits the weaker, nondominant side. For open-water swimming, this can lead to a more balanced and symmetrical pulling phase of the freestyle swim stroke. For the cyclist, this individual arm focus will be apparent when pulling up hard on the base bars, or cow horns, when climbing a steep hill.

Dumbbell Pullover

Posterior deltoid
Teres major
Pectoralis major
Latissimus dorsi
Serratus anterior

Execution

1. Using a stability ball for instability and activation of core muscle groups, hold a dumbbell with both hands.

2. Slide down so that your upper back is supported by the ball, with your back flat and your feet about shoulder-width apart.

3. Lower the dumbbell with your elbows slightly bent until it's even with your head. Focus on activating the muscles in your chest and upper back as you return the dumbbell to the starting position.

Muscles Involved

Primary: Pectoralis major

Secondary: Latissimus dorsi, teres major, pectoralis minor, posterior deltoid, serratus anterior, rhomboid major, rhomboid minor

Triathlon Focus

This basic exercise offers a variety of benefits for the triathlete. For swimming, it targets muscle groups used in the pulling phase of the stroke. It develops the muscles used when stretched out in the aero position when cycling with aerobars. The runner will benefit from being able to generate more propulsive force with the upper body when pumping her arms to tackle steep climbs or when sprinting to the finish line. For the runner, this enhanced upper-body balance and improved ability to drive with the arms will help during running surges late in a race or when charging uphill.

VARIATION

Bench Dumbbell Pullover

When first attempting the pullover movement, some athletes should use a stable surface such as a bench instead of the stability ball. Essentially, the exercise is performed in the same manner as with a stability ball but without the need to engage core muscle groups for enhanced stability, enabling the athlete to focus on the target muscle groups.

Chest Dip

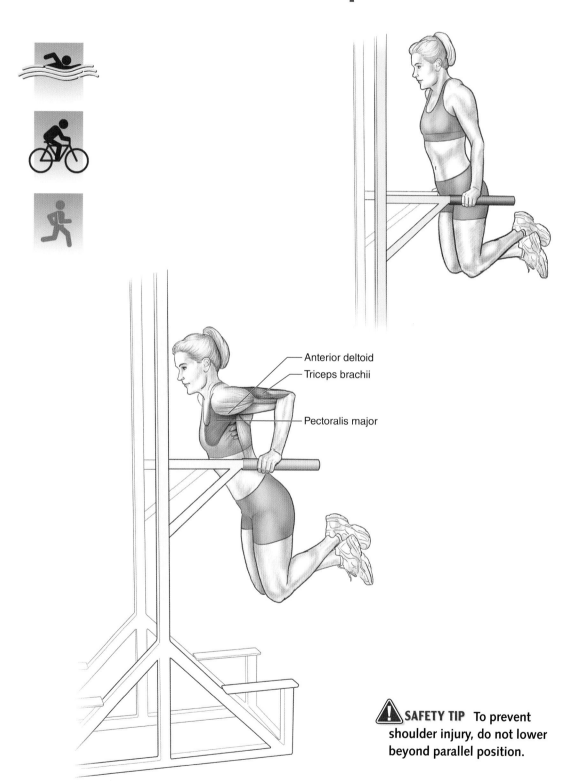

Anterior deltoid
Triceps brachii

Pectoralis major

⚠️ **SAFETY TIP** To prevent shoulder injury, do not lower beyond parallel position.

Execution

1. Using a dip bar or parallel bars, start with your arms supporting your weight, with elbows slightly bent.
2. Lower your body slowly until your upper arms are parallel to the floor, while leaning your torso slightly forward to better activate the chest muscles.
3. Press up to the starting position, keeping the arms slightly bent at completion. Repeat for the required number of reps.

Muscles Involved

Primary: Pectoralis major, triceps brachii

Secondary: Anterior deltoid

Triathlon Focus

The dip is a basic movement that offers a lot of bang for the buck when it comes to increasing upper-body strength and endurance. For the triathlete during the swim leg, the dip targets muscles critical for successful freestyle swimming, including the pectoralis major and the triceps brachii. For cycling, the dip will enable the triathlete to ride longer and more comfortably in the aerobars, as well as provide the athlete with an enhanced ability to climb in the standing position over short, steep hills.

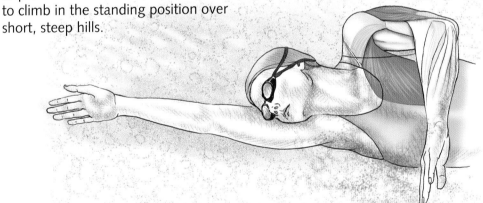

Standing Double-Arm Medicine Ball Throw-Down

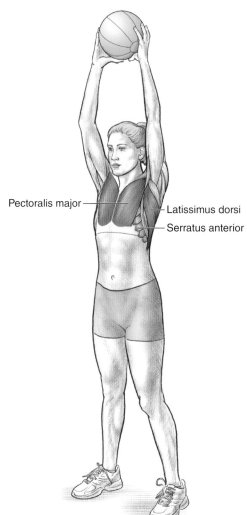

Pectoralis major

Latissimus dorsi

Serratus anterior

Execution

1. Choose a medicine ball of an appropriate weight. While standing on concrete or another hard surface, hold the ball with arms almost straight over your head.

2. With an explosive effort, throw the ball down to the ground roughly 12 to 15 inches (30 to 38 cm) in front of your toes.

3. Catch the ball as it bounces back up. Return to the starting position with the ball over your head, and repeat the movement for the required number of repetitions.

Muscles Involved

Primary: Pectoralis major, latissimus dorsi
Secondary: Serratus anterior

Triathlon Focus

This movement targets the muscle fibers that create explosive force and power in both the chest and upper back. It is an ideal exercise for the triathlete focused on freestyle swimming. Successful open-water swimming requires that the athlete establish good position with other swimmers of similar ability so as to conserve energy by drafting. This requires a quick start at the gun with a sprint. Explosive power is a key component of successful sprinting, and medicine ball work such as this addresses that need.

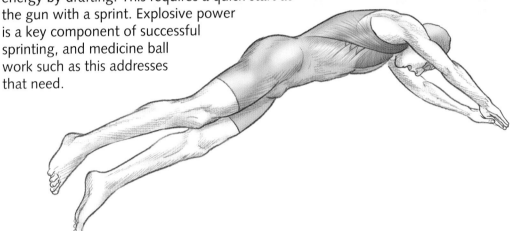

Stability Ball Dumbbell Fly

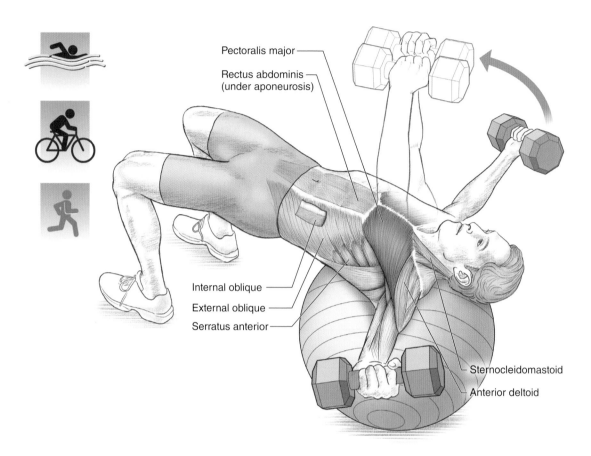

Pectoralis major

Rectus abdominis
(under aponeurosis)

Internal oblique

External oblique

Serratus anterior

Sternocleidomastoid

Anterior deltoid

Execution

1. With a dumbbell of the appropriate weight in each hand, sit on a stability ball and slide down on your back until your upper back is firmly balanced, with your feet flat on the floor and shoulder-width apart. Your back and neck should be straight.
2. Start with both dumbbells extended over your head, elbows slightly bent, and palms facing each other. Lower the dumbbells out to your sides. Focus on allowing the chest and anterior deltoid muscles to do the work.
3. As if hugging a large tree trunk, return to the starting position with a slow and controlled motion. Repeat for the required number of reps.

Muscles Involved

Primary: Pectoralis major

Secondary: Anterior deltoid, rectus abdominis, sternocleidomastoid, external oblique, internal oblique, serratus anterior

Triathlon Focus

Triathletes need to strengthen key upper-body muscles for stronger open-water swimming and greater stability on the bike when time trialing, especially over challenging hilly courses. The stability ball dumbbell fly offers a fantastic pectoralis major movement as well as the added benefit of increasing core strength and balance. For swimmers, this translates to a stronger and more explosive pull phase of the freestyle stroke. For cyclists, it enhances the ability to whip the bike back and forth in the case of an explosive climb or sprint to break away from a pack or drop an athlete who might be intentionally drafting off your wheel.

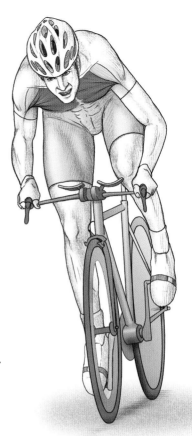

Incline Dumbbell Fly

Targeting a little more of the anterior deltoid and upper pectoral, the incline dumbbell fly is a slight variation recommended primarily for the more advanced strength training triathlete. The incline dumbbell fly may be performed on an incline bench or a stability ball.

Medicine Ball Push-Up

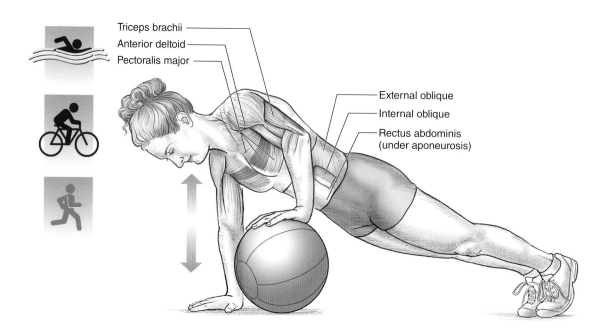

Triceps brachii
Anterior deltoid
Pectoralis major
External oblique
Internal oblique
Rectus abdominis (under aponeurosis)

Execution

1. With one hand on a medicine ball and the other on the floor, start in standard push-up position. Keep your body straight and your head in neutral position.
2. Lower your body until your chest almost touches the floor. Keep your body straight and your back flat.
3. Return to the starting position. The elbow of the hand on the medicine ball should be slightly bent; the other arm straightens nearly completely but does not lock at the elbow. Switch hands so the other hand is on the medicine ball, and perform this same sequence with the opposite arm. Instead of alternating hands, you may choose to perform a complete set with one arm then switch to the other.

Muscles Involved

Primary: Middle pectoralis major

Secondary: Triceps brachii, anterior deltoid, rectus abdominis, internal oblique, external oblique, serratus anterior

Triathlon Focus

This variation of the push-up engages core muscle groups as well as targets the upper body. This pushes muscles in a slightly different manner, which helps with balanced muscle development as well as adds variety to the resistance training program.

Like the traditional push-up, this exercise complements the freestyle swim stroke necessary for strong open-water swimming by enhancing the strength and endurance of the pectoralis major, anterior deltoid, and triceps brachii. For cycling and time trialing especially, stronger chest muscles and triceps facilitate a stronger overall foundation on the bike for more power generation when riding in the aero position.

"To core or not to core" is not the question but the answer. Triathletes train and race in three very different sports. Improvement in cardiorespiratory fitness is a given—the heart doesn't know or care whether you are running, biking, or swimming. The musculoskeletal system, on the other hand, may need more guidance on how to get stronger and stay healthy. The physical demands, including stress on the joints, muscles, tendons, ligaments, and bones, during triathlon training and racing are unique. With endurance activities, prolonged stress can lead to potential fatigue and biomechanical failure, with a subsequent decrease in performance and increase in risk of injury. Sport-specific training can be helpful for injury prevention and performance enhancement. Of equal if not greater importance is the value of core stability in building a strong foundation that helps develop biomechanical efficiency, create power, resist fatigue, and prevent injury.

What is core stability? The core can be defined as the region of the body that includes the bones of the hips, pelvis, and lower spine in conjunction with the muscles of the abdominal wall, pelvis, lower back, and diaphragm, which function together to stabilize the body as the lower and upper extremities move during activity. This lumbopelvic–hip complex is composed of both passive and active elements. The passive elements, including bones and ligamentous support of the lower spine, pelvis, and hip joint, are very strong and provide form and structure to the body. The active core muscles are the superficial and deep spinal extensor muscles, or paraspinals; abdominal muscles; pelvic floor muscles; and hip girdle muscles.

Coordinated contraction of the abdominal muscles against the solid abdominal organs forms a ball-like core region that functions as a stabilizing platform to maintain an upright posture. Any activity is initiated by this core contraction. Core stability is essential for the transfer of force and power from the ground across the body and to the extremities.

A second active component of core stability is the complex neuromuscular coordination of both passive and active elements by the brain and spinal cord. Anticipation of activity or preparation for movement requires a coordinated sequence of muscle contractions to occur. Similarly, postural adjustments or control of balance depends on proper core functioning. These so-called trunk neurological reflexes are mostly automatic, but it has been shown that people can use core training to improve their response to sudden load changes. It is also known that not one single muscle or structure can provide significant stability to the core at any given time. The interactions of many components, both passive and active, change with each activity, and that creates the ability to swim, bike, and run.

To better understand the function of core stability and how it affects every movement in the body, let's examine the concept of the kinetic chain and the exercise concepts that improve its function, including open- and closed-chain kinetic exercises. *Kinetic chain* is a term describing a series of events in the musculoskeletal system that allow for movement and power generation. These actions require a coordinated process that relies on strength, flexibility, and range of motion in all parts of the body to allow an athlete to swim, bike, and run. Joint motion and subsequent power generation come from an initial contraction of the core muscles. This acts as the foundation on which all other activity occurs. In swimming, the catch phase and subsequent arm pull are aided by the contraction of the core muscles. This provides the anchor for the latissimus dorsi and shoulder and arm muscles to pull against and cause forward motion. During biking, if it were not for a stable pelvis and spine, an athlete could not maintain balance and produce force with the pressing down and pulling up of the pedals. Similarly as the runner transfers weight from one leg to the other, a stable pelvis and spine assist in shock absorption, force production, and injury prevention by maintaining proper running mechanics.

Bony Structures of the Core

The bony anatomy of the core consists of the upper portion of the femurs, or thighbones, which form a ball-and-socket joint with the cup formed in the pelvis, called the acetabulum (figure 7.1). Unlike the shoulder joint, the hip joint is very stable. A strong ligamentous support surrounds the joint, creating what is referred to as a constrained joint. This design allows for motion, weight transmission, and stability. Dislocation of the hip is an uncommon occurrence and is usually caused by significant trauma.

The pelvis is made up of six bones: the ilium, ischium, and pubis, one on each side. These bones are tightly bound together, forming a circular platform with the sacrum at the back of the pelvis to protect internal organs and support the lower extremities. Weight-bearing forces that occur with impact loading or pushing activities pass through the hip joints and are distributed over the pelvis and dissipated to the spine.

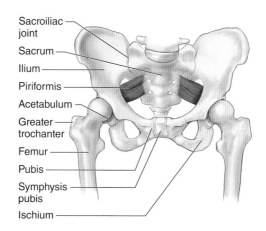

Sacroiliac joint
Sacrum
Ilium
Piriformis
Acetabulum
Greater trochanter
Femur
Pubis
Symphysis pubis
Ischium

Figure 7.1   Bony structures of the pelvis.

Muscles of the Core

The top portion of the ilium, the iliac crest, serves as the origin of the hip abductor muscu-lature including the tensor fasciae latae, gluteus medius, and gluteus minimus (figure 7.2). These muscles pull the leg away from the midline of the body and help stabilize the pelvis. The gluteus maximus originates from the back of the iliac crest and sacrum. It inserts into the posterior portion of the upper femur and is the main hip extensor. The front of the pelvis, the pubis, is the origin of the adductor group of muscles, those that pull the leg toward the midline of the body, discussed in more detail a little later. The ischium is the origin for the hamstring muscles and is referred to as the sit bone because this is actually what we sit on and why a good fit for a bike seat is so important. We all know what it is like when that fit isn't right!

The muscular anatomy of the core can be divided into groups based on the motions they produce or resist. The large superficial muscles of the hip and trunk are best suited to provide core stability, but smaller muscles referred to as intrinsics play a significant role and should not be disregarded.

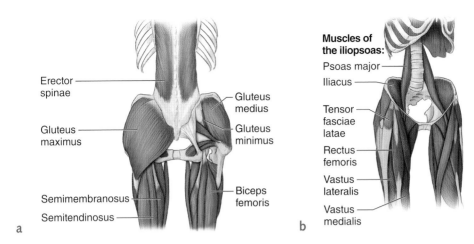

Figure 7.2 Muscles of the lower core and upper leg: *(a)* back; *(b)* front.

When acting in isolation, the rectus abdominis (figure 7.3a) and transversus abdominis (figure 7.3b) of the abdominals initiate and produce trunk flexion (bending forward). The erector spinae and multifidus of the back (figure 7.4), and the gluteus maximus and hamstrings of the hips and legs cause hip and trunk extension, or backward bending. Coordinated co-contraction stabilizes the trunk. Force generation through the gluteus maximus to the lower extremities allows for activities such as running and jumping.

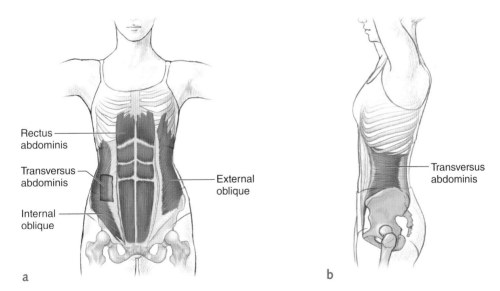

Figure 7.3 Abdominal muscles: *(a)* front view, showing the rectus abdominis and external and internal obliques; *(b)* side view, showing the transversus abdominis.

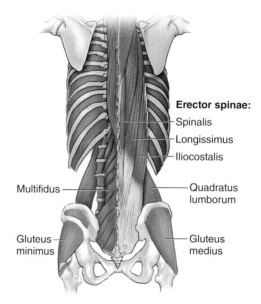

Erector spinae:
- Spinalis
- Longissimus
- Iliocostalis

Multifidus

Quadratus lumborum

Gluteus minimus

Gluteus medius

Figure 7.4   Core muscles of the back.

Muscles that control motion from side to side include the gluteus medius, gluteus minimus, and quadratus lumborum. In isolation, the gluteus medius and gluteus minimus abduct the leg away from the body. When the leg is planted on the ground during walking or running, these muscles hold the pelvis level and maintain lower-extremity alignment. The quadratus lumborum is very active during all upright motion and is a chief stabilizer of the spine. Weaknesses in these areas are often a prime factor in the development of overuse injuries in the lower extremity seen in runners.

The group of hip adductors, those that pull the leg toward the midline of the body, include the adductor magnus, adductor longus, adductor brevis, and pectineus. These adductors, along with the hip external rotators, superior and inferior gemelli, quadratus femoris, obturator externus, and obturator internus play a secondary role in core stability. These muscles are covered in more detail in chapter 9.

There are many passive and dynamic parts of this system, including bones, muscles, and neurological system coordination, that help maintain upright posture and active body motion. Weakness in any component can lead to excessive force transmission to the spine, which can result in injury. Loss of stability from core dysfunction can lead to overuse injuries in the lower extremities. Loss of force transmission could potentially lead to decreased performance in both training and racing; controversy still exists.

Exercises for the Core

The core is often thought of as simply the muscles in the abdominal region, sides, and lower back. In actuality, the core involves these areas as well as other supporting muscles such as the glutes and lats. A coordinated, finely tuned effort from these muscles supports the spine and sets the foundation for balanced movement.

Although it's not uncommon to hear someone boast of how many sit-ups he can do at one time, the truth is the muscles of the core are like any other muscle in the body and adapt similarly to training stresses. Therefore, most of the core exercises explained in this book are meant to be done 2 or 3 days per week, for two or three sets of 10 to 15 challenging repetitions.

To maximize core stability, you need to develop core strength. This is accomplished by performing specific exercises that involve core muscle activation and are performed with sport-specific actions in mind. A basic abdominal crunch does not simulate the activities performed in triathlon. However holding a position such as a plank can simulate riding in the aerobars. The longer you can stay there, the more aerodynamic you will be and the less fatigue you'll feel coming off the bike and starting the run.

The following exercises are done using your own body weight to produce strength and endurance. As strength improves, attempt to hold each position for a greater amount of time or to perform more repetitions. These exercises will help you develop a strong functional core that can lead to injury-free training and racing.

Plank

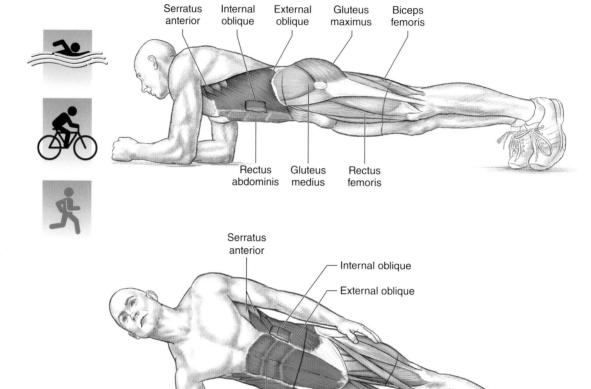

Execution

1. Start in a prone position, face down and back straight, with weight rested on forearms and toes.
2. Engaging the entire core area and keeping the body flat, hold this position for 15 to 30 seconds, depending on your level of fitness.
3. Rotate to face left, supporting yourself on your right forearm and the side of your right foot. Keep your left arm at your side, or for added difficulty, point it straight up. Hold this position for 15 to 30 seconds.
4. Return to the forward position, then rotate to the other side, using the same technique as described in step 3. If you are more advanced, hold the forward position for 15 to 30 seconds before rotating to the other side.

Muscles Involved

Primary: Rectus abdominis, external oblique, internal oblique, transversus abdominis

Secondary: Serratus anterior, rectus femoris, gluteus maximus, gluteus medius, hamstrings (biceps femoris, semitendinosus, semimembranosus)

Triathlon Focus

The plank is an extremely effective core development exercise and should be integrated into every triathlete's strength training routine. Swimmers and cyclists in particular require stronger muscles that stabilize the body when in a horizontal plane, including freestyle swimming and laying out on aerobars.

The key to performing the plank exercise is to keep the body rigid and the head in a neutral position. If the hips begin to drop, you'll need to focus on activating the muscle groups to bring them back into line or discontinue the exercise until your endurance improves. It's recommended that you start with 15 seconds in each position (front facing and side facing) and work up to holding each position for up to 1 minute.

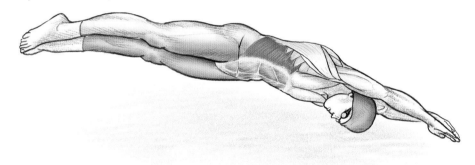

V-Sit

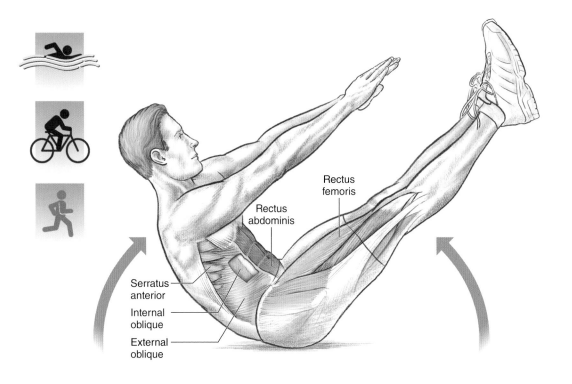

Rectus femoris

Rectus abdominis

Serratus anterior

Internal oblique

External oblique

Execution

1. Start by lying flat on your back on a mat or other soft surface.
2. Simultaneously raise your upper body and your legs, bending at the hips, forming a V shape.
3. Return to the start position, and repeat the movement for the required number of repetitions.

Muscles Involved

Primary: Rectus abdominis

Secondary: External oblique, internal oblique, transversus abdominis, serratus anterior, rectus femoris, iliopsoas

Triathlon Focus

The V-sit is an advanced core strength exercise that engages key muscle groups in the abdominal region, hip region, and upper leg.

The swimmer will benefit from lower abdominal strengthening and hip area strengthening with an improved kicking motion. Cyclists will be more comfortable during extended time in the aero position while also benefitting from strengthened hip flexor and rectus femoris muscles, important for pulling up or unweighting the pedals during the 7 to 11 o'clock phase of the pedal-stroke cycle.

Add intensity to this exercise by lowering the legs and upper body almost to the ground, but not all the way, maintaining constant muscle activation.

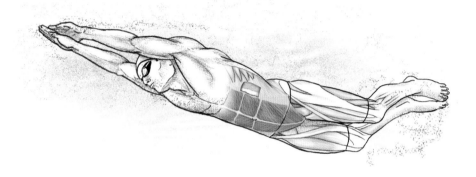

VARIATION

V-Sit With Weights

Add intensity to the V-sit by holding a medicine ball or other weight at the chest and then extending it toward the legs during each repetition.

Flutter Kick

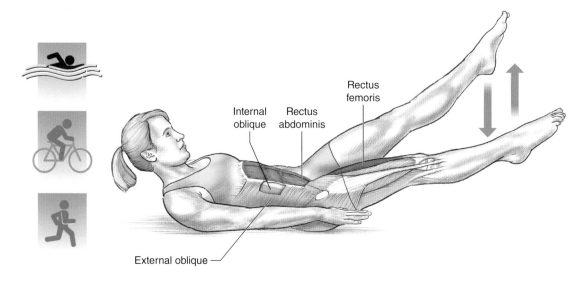

Rectus femoris

Internal oblique

Rectus abdominis

External oblique

Execution

1. Start by lying on your back with your toes pointed and your arms at your sides.
2. Gently lift your shoulders and hands slightly off the ground, engaging your core, while also bringing your feet 12 to 16 inches (30 to 40 cm) off the ground, keeping your toes pointed.
3. From this position, kick your legs up and down (flutter kick). Focus on keeping your toes pointed.
4. Perform these kicks for 15 to 30 seconds, working toward the goal of 60 seconds, resting 30 to 60 seconds between each set.

Muscles Involved

Primary: Rectus abdominis, rectus femoris

Secondary: External oblique, internal oblique, transversus abdominis, iliopsoas

Triathlon Focus

The flutter kick activates key muscle groups, including the lower rectus abdominis and the rectus femoris, used when kicking during the freestyle swim stroke. In addition, performing this exercise and pointing your toes can improve ankle flexibility, a key area negatively affected by excessive run training. A key to performing this exercise is to focus on keeping the lower back flat with the help of the abdominal musculature. Keep your toes pointed as well, promoting greater ankle flexibility and better foot position for more propulsive kicking during the freestyle stroke cycle.

Stability Ball Crunch

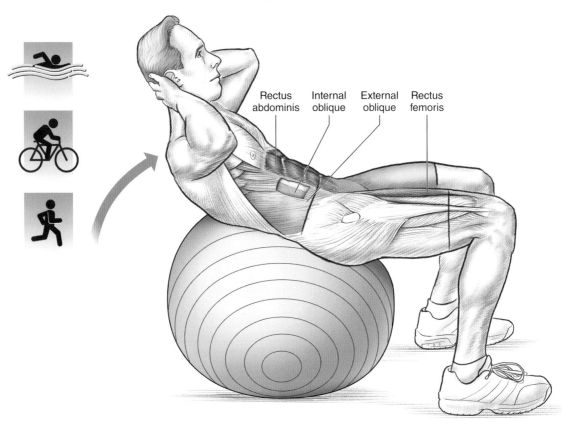

Rectus abdominis, Internal oblique, External oblique, Rectus femoris

Execution

1. Start this exercise with the stability ball positioned in the middle of your back. Plant your feet on the floor about shoulder-width apart.

2. Support your head with your hands in a neutral position, but don't pull your head up with your hands as this places undue strain on your neck.

3. Raise your chest and shoulders toward the ceiling. Focus on isolating and engaging your abdominal muscles. Hold the crunch for a few seconds when you near full contraction.

4. Lower slowly to the starting position, and repeat for the required number of repetitions.

Muscles Involved

Primary: Rectus abdominis

Secondary: External oblique, internal oblique, transversus abdominis, rectus femoris

Triathlon Focus

The stability ball crunch is a safe and effective core strengthening exercise that should be a staple in your triathlon core strength training program. It's easy to perform and can be adjusted to suit your current fitness level.

Always focus on proper form and on isolating your abdominal muscles when you perform this exercise. Keep your feet flat and your quads parallel to the ground as you balance yourself on the ball.

Working on the core offers an indirect boost to swimming, cycling, and running performance by enhancing the strength and stability of muscles responsible for balance. That sets the foundation for all movement. The stability ball crunch engages the abdominal region in a manner nonspecific to swimming, cycling, and running, but nevertheless it is effective in building strength and endurance and is recommended for all athletes.

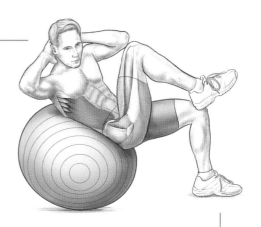

VARIATION

Stability Ball Crunch With Trunk Rotation

By incorporating a twisting motion and alternating side to side with each crunch, you'll target the internal and external obliques, enhancing your ability to rotate the torso.

Russian Twist

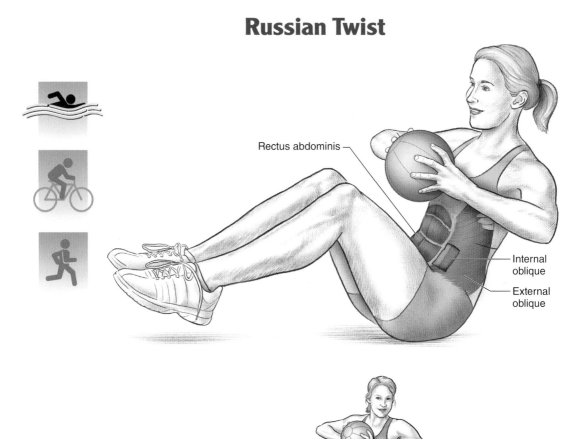

Rectus abdominis

Internal oblique

External oblique

Execution

1. Sitting on the ground with your knees bent, hold an appropriately weighted medicine ball, one that enables you to perform 10 to 15 repetitions with considerable effort, to your chest with both hands.

2. Gradually lean back so that your torso forms approximately a 45-degree angle to the floor. Raise your feet 3 to 6 inches (7.5 to 15 cm) off the ground.

3. Using only your trunk muscles, rotate from side to side. Repeat this movement for 10 to 15 repetitions.

Muscles Involved

Primary: Rectus abdominis, external oblique, internal oblique

Secondary: Psoas major

Triathlon Focus

The Russian twist is an excellent exercise for targeting the obliques and enhancing your ability to rotate at the hips. This is especially important in freestyle swimming since core strength is critical for maintaining a streamlined position in the water. As the leading hand enters the water and reaches before the catch, the core is engaged as the pulling motion is initiated, helping to whip the hips into proper alignment for maximum acceleration and streamlining.

Stability Ball Prayer Roll

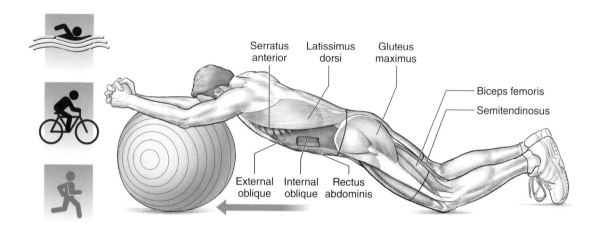

Execution

1. Start on your knees while resting your forearms on a stability ball.
2. Slowly push the ball away, using your forearms to support your weight until you achieve an outstretched position suitable for your current level of fitness.
3. After a brief pause, roll the ball back to the starting position. Repeat for 10 to 15 repetitions.

Muscles Involved

Primary: Rectus abdominis, external oblique, internal oblique, transversus abdominis

Secondary: Latissimus dorsi, serratus anterior, gluteus maximus, hamstrings (biceps femoris, semitendinosus, semimembranosus)

Triathlon Focus

This is a very effective core strengthening exercise, targeting muscles in the abdominal region as well as in the upper and lower back. Its application to freestyle swimming is very apparent, as it specifically addresses many of the muscle groups used in the underwater pulling phase of the stroke. And it'll help the triathlete outstretched on a tri bike in the aero position ride longer with greater comfort.

Reverse Crunch

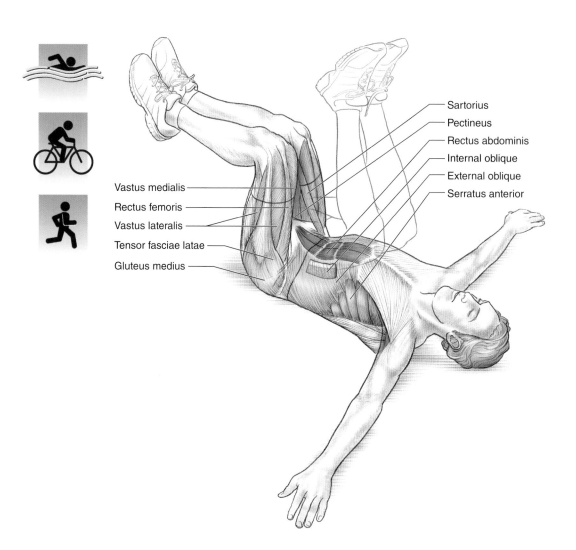

Sartorius
Pectineus
Rectus abdominis
Internal oblique
External oblique
Serratus anterior

Vastus medialis
Rectus femoris
Vastus lateralis
Tensor fasciae latae
Gluteus medius

Execution

1. Lie on your back with your upper legs perpendicular to the ground and your lower legs parallel to the ground.
2. Stabilize your upper body by stretching your arms out to your sides, palms flat on the ground.
3. Focus on engaging the lower abdominal muscles as you lift your pelvis off the floor, bringing your knees toward your chest.
4. Lower your pelvis to the starting position. Repeat for the required number of repetitions.

Muscles Involved

Primary: Rectus abdominis

Secondary: External oblique, internal oblique, transversus abdominis, serratus anterior, quadriceps (rectus femoris, vastus lateralis, vastus medialis, vastus intermedius), hip flexors (including the gluteus medius, tensor fasciae latae, sartorius, pectineus)

Triathlon Focus

It is important for the triathlete to develop the muscles of the lower abdominal region as they are constantly engaged in each of the three disciplines. This particular exercise offers a safe and effective way to strengthen these muscles by isolating the area for maximum engagement while limiting the likelihood of cheating during its execution. From the freestyle kick in open-water swimming to hard uphill charges both on the bike and on the run, strong core muscles will assist you in maintaining proper form while pushing toward the finish line.

Back Extension Press-Up

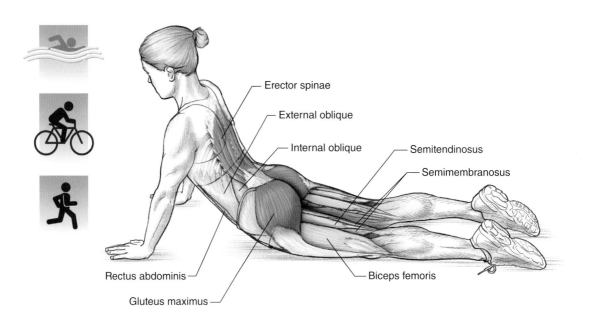

Erector spinae

External oblique

Internal oblique

Semitendinosus

Semimembranosus

Rectus abdominis

Biceps femoris

Gluteus maximus

Execution

1. Start on the ground in the push-up position, face down and back flat.
2. Slowly push up with the arms until only your torso is off the ground. Your legs stay flat on the floor.
3. Hold this position for 10 to 15 seconds. Focus on activating the muscles of the lower back and glutes.
4. Return to the starting position, and repeat for the required number of repetitions.

Muscles Involved

Primary: Erector spinae, gluteus maximus

Secondary: Hamstrings (biceps femoris, semitendinosus, semimembranosus), rectus abdominis, external oblique, internal oblique

Triathlon Focus

Core strengthening exercises are critical for triathlon success in many ways. Unfortunately, many athletes overemphasize the abdominal region and neglect the important muscles in the lower back and buttocks, ultimately leading to muscular imbalances and further increasing the risk of injury during repetitive-motion activities.

The back extension press-up is a simple exercise that offers a huge return on investment in terms of developing those key back muscles to stabilize the pelvic region. This is especially important for the running leg of the triathlon as a misaligned pelvic region can adversely affect the runner's gait, leading to other biomechanical inefficiencies and potential injury.

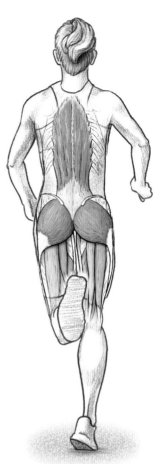

BACK AND NECK

Neck and back pain will affect approximately 60 to 80 percent of the U.S. population during their lifetimes. So why do we spend so little time trying to keep our necks and backs healthy and strong? Throughout our lives we have heard phrases such as "watch your back" or that someone's got his "back against the wall." These simple words emphasize the potential vulnerability of the area. The perceived fear of exercising the neck and back has led us to ignore a prime area where we could dramatically decrease the chance of injury and disability.

The physical demands we put on our bodies during triathlon participation place us at risk for injury. Whether injury is caused by poor technique, fatigue, or equipment issues, endurance training and racing place highly repetitive stresses on all our tissues, which can lead to breakdown and injury. Lack of body rotation during swimming forces the athlete to use excessive rotation of the head, which can cause stress to the neck and result in pain and stiffness. Improper bike fit, poor riding position, or even just riding too many hours in the saddle can lead to neck and lower back pain. Running induces high-impact forces on the spine and its supporting tissues. Couple this with worn-out sneakers and bad running form, and back and neck issues are soon to follow. This group of injuries can be described as strains or mechanical pain. Neck and back strains can be caused by an injury to one or multiple structures of the spine including bones, tendons, ligaments, discs, and muscles. This should be differentiated from neurological or radicular pain in which nerve irritation produces a constellation of symptoms including pain that is felt more so in the leg and arm than in the back or neck, respectively.

To better understand the importance of the neck and back and their relationship to health and function, we will discuss each anatomical component separately and convince you that an ounce of prevention with a well-designed strength and flexibility training program can minimize the chance of injury and improve performance.

Bony Structures of the Back and Neck

The core structures of the neck and back are the bones that make up the spinal column. The spine is composed of 33 vertebrae: 7 cervical (C1–C7), 12 thoracic (T1–T12), 5 lumbar (L1–L5), 5 fused sacral vertebrae that form the sacrum, and 4 coccygeal bones that form the tailbone (figure 8.1).

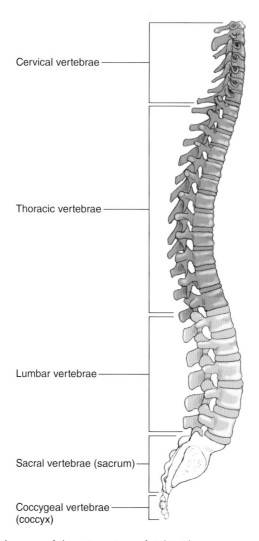

Cervical vertebrae

Thoracic vertebrae

Lumbar vertebrae

Sacral vertebrae (sacrum)

Coccygeal vertebrae
(coccyx)

Figure 8.1　Regions and curves of the spine, view of right side.

Each vertebra has two essential components: an anterior segment (the vertebral body) and a posterior part (the vertebral or neural arch). Each vertebral body is stacked on another to form the length of the spinal column (figure 8.2). Intervertebral discs separate the vertebral bodies, except for the sacrum and coccygeal bones. The vertebral arches attach to one another via two joints, one on each side, called the facets. A series of ligaments that run the length of the spinal column help connect each segment, creating a support column that holds the head and trunk upright and protects the spinal cord and its nerve roots.

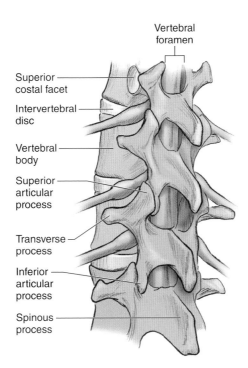

Vertebral
foramen

Superior
costal facet

Intervertebral
disc

Vertebral
body

Superior
articular
process

Transverse
process

Inferior
articular
process

Spinous
process

Figure 8.2   Vertebrae along the spine.

The intervertebral disc and each adjacent vertebra create a motion segment. By them-selves they have little motion, but as you stack multiple segments on top of each other, a flexible column is created. At the core of this motion is the intervertebral disc. Think of it as a jelly donut that has a fibrous ring, annulus fibrosus, surrounding the nucleus pulposus, a jelly-like substance, in its center (figure 8.3). Ninety percent of the nucleus is composed of water, creating an incompressible pillow.

The disc performs two functions, motion and shock absorption. Motion of the spine occurs from the interplay between the annulus fibrosus and the nucleus pulposus. Vertical pressure exerted on the spine with impact loading is resisted by the relatively incompressible nucleus pulposus contained within the fibrous ring. As early as the 20s and 30s, degenerative changes can occur in the disc and in the facet joints. Loss of water in the nucleus pulposus and breakdown of the collagen fiber structure of the annulus fibrosus can decrease the shock absorption ability of the vertebra and place it at risk for disc herniation. In this condition, the jelly escapes the confines of the fibrous ring and potentially presses on the spinal cord or one of its nerves, causing pain that can radiate down a leg or arm, depending on the disc level. Deterioration of the facet joints, including loss of the cartilage lining, and stiffness or fibrosis of the surrounding ligaments can cause pain and a loss of motion about the spine.

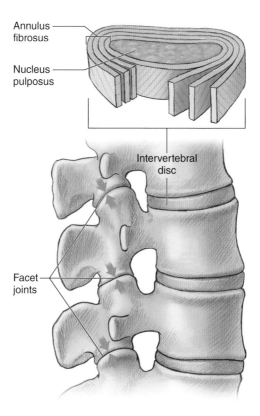

Figure 8.3   Facet joints and intervertebral discs, with a detail of an intervertebral disc.

The normal spine has an S-shaped curve when viewed from the side (see figure 8.1) and looks straight when viewed from the front. These curves develop in childhood. We are born with a C-shaped spine, called kyphosis. (The upper back looks posteriorly convex when viewed from the side.) As a baby starts to crawl and lift her head, cervical lordosis develops. (The upper back looks anteriorly convex when viewed from the side.) With continued muscular development and the onset of walking, more weight is distributed onto the spine, and lumbar lordosis is created. The mature S-shaped spine allows for even distribution of weight and for balance and flexibility of the spine.

Muscles of the Back and Neck

Everything described so far is a passive structural element of the spine, but what makes it move? A group of deep, strong muscles in the back including the erector spinae (figure 8.4), multifidus (figure 8.5), and intertransversarii muscles control the movements of the lower and middle spine.

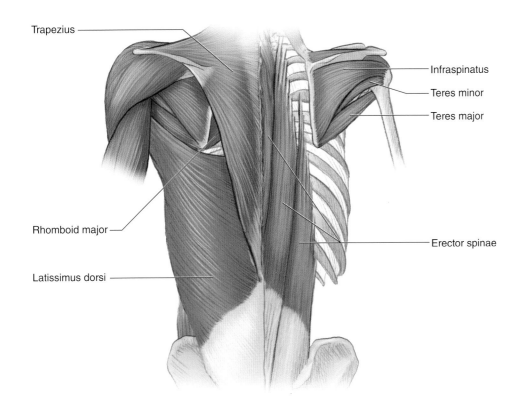

Figure 8.4 Muscles of the back: trapezius, rhomboid major, latissimus dorsi, infraspinatus, teres minor, teres major, and erector spinae.

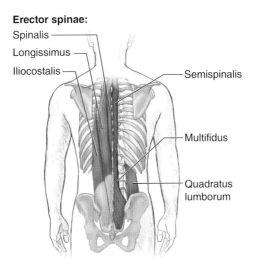

Figure 8.5 Deeper back muscles, including the multifidus and semispinalis.

Upper-back and cervical motion are controlled by similar muscles but also by a large group of smaller neck muscles (figure 8.6) including the sternocleidomastoid, scalene, and splenius capitis, to name a few.

Other muscles on the back that contribute to motion about the spine include the trapezius; the latissimus dorsi; and the deep scapular rotator, the levator scapulae.

Motions that occur about the spine are flexion and extension (bending forward and backward); side bending, or lateral flexion; and rotation. In the cervical spine the majority of rotation occurs at the uppermost vertebral bodies, C1 and C2; flexion and extension occur at the lower cervical vertebrae, C5 and C6. In the lumbar spine, rotation is somewhat evenly distributed among all vertebrae, but flexion and extension occur in the L3–L4 and L4–L5 regions. At these sites, most degenerative changes occur due to their increased mobility.

Flexion of the spine occurs through the action of the anterior muscles of the abdomen and rectus abdominis. Extension of the spine is performed by a muscle group called the erector spinae. It is made up of three separate muscles—the iliocostalis, longissimus, and spinalis—that run vertically along the spine from the sacrum to the cervical region. Some of the fibers are also continuous with the gluteus maximus. Their main function is to stabilize and extend the spine.

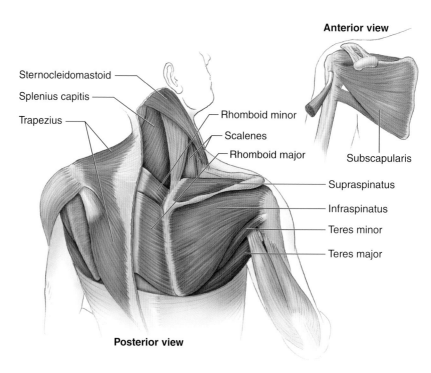

Figure 8.6 Muscles of the neck, upper back, and rotator cuff.

Lateral spine rotation and side bending are performed by the oblique muscles of the abdomen in conjunction with isolated contraction of the erector spinae group. The intertransversarii muscles are small muscles that run between the transverse processes of each vertebra. Their location on the spine also assists in lateral flexion of the spine.

The multifidus muscle is a very thin deep muscle of the back that runs from the sacrum up into the cervical region in the groove next to the spinous process, that bony prominence you can feel on your back, of each vertebra. The main function of the multifidus is to stabilize each joint segment of the spine.

In the cervical region, the sternocleidomastoid on each side of the neck is responsible for rotation and side bending. The scalene muscles, three on each side, perform lateral bending of the head. Both muscle groups also facilitate respiration, an important function in exercise. The trapezius, by virtue of its attachments to the base of the skull, scapula, and spine, links the neck to the rest of the body and assists with extension, rotation, and neck bending.

Exercises for the Back and Neck

For muscular endurance and strength development, strive to complete two to four sets of 10 to 15 repetitions for the exercises in this chapter. To maximize the benefit of each set, choose a weight that challenges you to complete the final repetitions. Research shows that resting 3 to 5 minutes between sets might be best for maximum strength development, and shorter rest intervals of up to 60 seconds elicit greater gains in muscular endurance. Depending on the intensity of the exercise and the relative difficulty of completing each set without going to failure, it's recommended that triathletes target a rest interval of 1 to 2 minutes between sets of moderate intensity.

The muscles of the back and neck are often ignored during training but physically taxed during racing and even during normal activities of daily living, such as sitting behind a desk hunched over a computer. To prevent injury to the low back and cervical region, you need to engage in strength training of this area as well as overall core and abdominal training.

The back especially requires an adequate warm-up period before you begin a strength training program. Because the back is a link to the upper and lower extremities, activities such as rowing or using an elliptical trainer are great for warming up. Increasing heart rate brings blood flow to all regions of the body. As core temperature rises, muscles, tendons, and ligaments are more receptive and compliant to the stresses placed on them. A proper warm-up period should entail low-level exercise in which you can easily hold a conversation, your heart rate is in the lower aerobic range, and you break a light sweat. Once this is accomplished, begin strength training. The exercises that follow will help develop a strong and healthy back and neck.

Floor Bridge

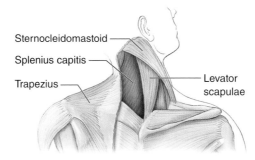

⚠️ **SAFETY TIP** This exercise requires extreme caution. Be sure your neck muscles are warmed up before performing this exercise. Don't attempt to engage the neck muscles beyond your comfort level. Never extend back to the top of your head or extremely arch your neck.

Execution

1. Start by lying on your back on the floor, with your knees bent and feet flat.
2. Gently press back on the floor with your head as you slowly raise your body and shoulders, engaging the muscles in the back of the neck. This should take 3 to 4 seconds.
3. Slowly roll back to the starting position, and repeat for the required number of repetitions.

Muscles Involved

Primary: Splenius capitis

Secondary: Trapezius, levator scapulae, erector spinae, posterior sternocleidomastoid

Triathlon Focus

The very nature of riding in the aero position on a tri bike forces you to extend your neck upward as you look at the road. The more aggressive your aerodynamic riding position, the more you need to look up and engage the muscles in the back of the neck. After a few hours in the saddle, your 10-pound (4.5 kg) head gets pretty heavy, and neck fatigue and stiffness can begin to settle in.

For the open-water swimmer, sighting the buoys requires frequent head-up, lifeguard-style strokes to maintain a proper course. This also places a lot of stress on the back of the neck. Supplementary strength training such as the floor bridge will help alleviate neck fatigue and soreness.

Lat Pull-Down

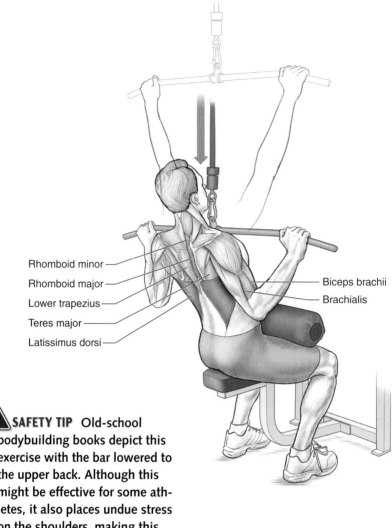

Rhomboid minor

Rhomboid major

Lower trapezius

Teres major

Latissimus dorsi

Biceps brachii

Brachialis

⚠ **SAFETY TIP** Old-school bodybuilding books depict this exercise with the bar lowered to the upper back. Although this might be effective for some athletes, it also places undue stress on the shoulders, making this technique ill advised.

Execution

1. Sit down at a lat pull-down machine so your legs are under the support pads, bracing your body. With your arms at full extension, grab the bar with an overhand grip (palms facing out), hands a little wider than shoulder-width apart.

2. Start each repetition by pulling the bar toward your upper chest, in a slow and controlled motion, until the bar is under your chin.

3. Slowly return the bar to starting position, with your arms fully extended. Repeat for the required number or repetitions.

Muscles Involved

Primary: Latissimus dorsi

Secondary: Lower trapezius, rhomboid major, rhomboid minor, teres major, biceps brachii, brachialis

Triathlon Focus

Similar in focus to the pull-up, the lat pull-down has the advantage of offering variable resistance and is a great alternative and starting point for athletes who cannot perform repetitions using their body weight or for very strong athletes who require loads that only a weight stack can offer.

As with the pull-up, this exercise is a multijoint mover that develops most of the pulling muscles of the upper body and benefits the triathlete through increased strength, stability, and endurance in that muscle region. The most direct application is for the swimming leg, but triathletes with strong upper backs will also notice positive results for the cycling and running legs as well.

We recommend that athletes start developing strength with this exercise, performing several sets of 10 to 12 repetitions with a challenging weight before moving on to the more difficult pull-up exercise.

Standing Straight-Arm Pull-Down

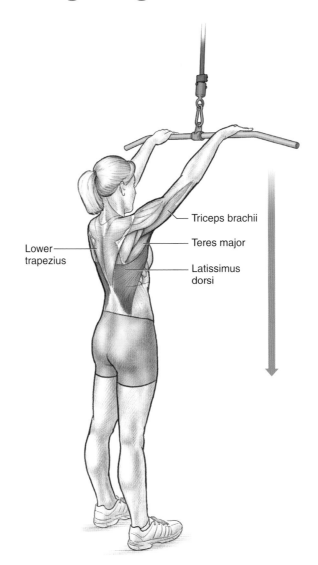

Triceps brachii

Teres major

Lower trapezius

Latissimus dorsi

Execution

1. Standing with a straight back, face the pulley machine.

2. Bending your arms ever so slightly, place your palms on the top of the bar to start the movement.

3. Maintaining the proper elbow position (high and flexed slightly), press the bar down in an arching movement to your upper thighs, almost touching them. Focus on engaging the latissimus dorsi muscles in the back throughout the movement.

4. Slowly return the bar to the starting position, and repeat for the required number of repetitions.

Muscles Involved

Primary: Latissimus dorsi, pectoralis major

Secondary: Lower trapezius, teres major, triceps brachii

Triathlon Focus

This exercise primarily benefits the swimming leg of the triathlon and can be incorporated into a triathlete's dryland resistance training routine. The overhead starting position closely mimics the initial pulling phase of the freestyle swim stroke, initiated after the hand enters the water with a catch. It then targets each muscle group as they'll be activated in the actual swim stroke up until the recovery phase.

When performing this exercise, focus on engaging the latissimus dorsi through most of the movement, with a slight shift in emphasis to the triceps brachii near the end of the movement. Keep the body still and avoid any jerking movements, which is cheating and negates the full effect of the exercise.

Pull-Up

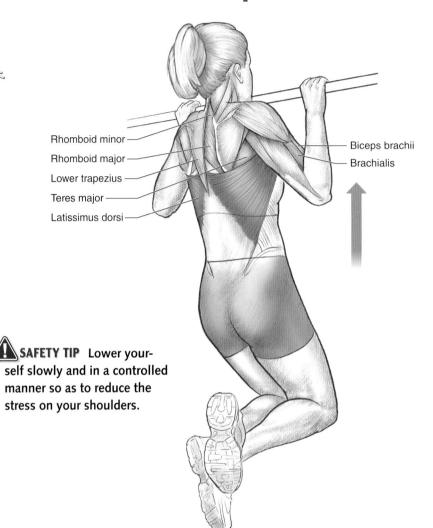

Rhomboid minor

Rhomboid major

Lower trapezius

Teres major

Latissimus dorsi

Biceps brachii

Brachialis

SAFETY TIP Lower yourself slowly and in a controlled manner so as to reduce the stress on your shoulders.

Execution

1. Hold the pull-up bar with an overhand grip, palms facing forward.
2. Bend your knees and cross your ankles for lower-body stability and to prevent rocking back and forth.
3. From a fully extended hanging position, pull your body up, bringing your upper chest to the bar.
4. Lower yourself slowly, and repeat for the required number of repetitions.

Muscles Involved

Primary: Latissimus dorsi

Secondary: Lower trapezius, rhomboid major, rhomboid minor, teres major, biceps brachii, brachialis

Triathlon Focus

You've probably dreaded performing pull-ups since you were in high-school gym class. However the pull-up is one of the most effective and all-encompassing upper-body exercises you can do to improve your pulling strength and develop your back muscles.

The most direct application for the triathlete is in swimming as this exercise targets muscles used in each phase of the freestyle swim stroke. Cyclists will enjoy the enhanced stability they feel when riding in the aero base and out of the saddle, while runners will be able to generate additional momentum with the arms when driving up a steep hill.

Consistency is the key to increasing your pull-up count. If at first it's difficult for you to complete a few repetitions, have someone assist you by holding your feet and helping you up. Once you can perform sets of 12 to 15 repetitions on your own, consider adding weight, in the form of a dumbbell, to be held between your crossed feet.

Chin-Up

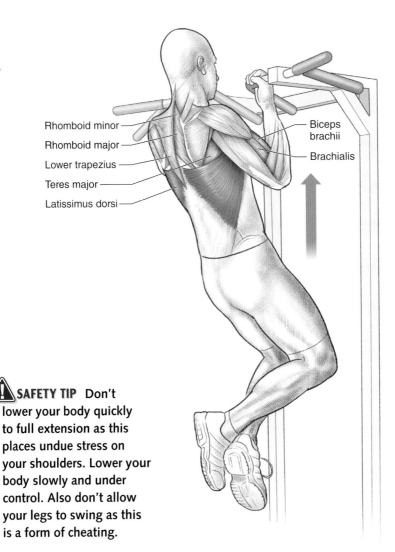

Rhomboid minor

Rhomboid major

Lower trapezius

Teres major

Latissimus dorsi

Biceps brachii

Brachialis

⚠ SAFETY TIP Don't lower your body quickly to full extension as this places undue stress on your shoulders. Lower your body slowly and under control. Also don't allow your legs to swing as this is a form of cheating.

Execution

1. Grab the chin-up bar with your palms facing you. Bend your knees and cross your ankles to stabilize your lower body.

2. From a fully extended position, gently raise your body, pulling your upper chest to the bar with the goal of pulling your chin over the bar for each repetition.

3. Lower to the starting position slowly and under control. Repeat for the required number of repetitions.

Muscles Involved

Primary: Latissimus dorsi

Secondary: Biceps brachii, brachialis, lower trapezius, rhomboid major, rhomboid minor, teres major

Triathlon Focus

A close cousin to the pull-up in form and function, the chin-up does more to emphasize the elbow flexors, including the biceps brachii and brachialis, while also developing the latissimus dorsi, the large muscle in the upper back.

Specific to the needs of the triathlon swimmer in particular, this exercise helps develop muscles necessary for a strong and consistent pull phase of the freestyle stroke. Cyclists benefit from this exercise by exhibiting greater stability and control of the bike when riding on the aero bars, and runners will like the additional push a strong upper back and arms offer during hard uphill charges.

Seated Double-Arm Machine Row

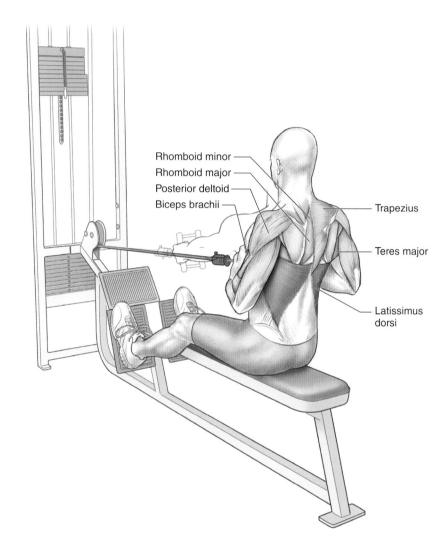

Rhomboid minor
Rhomboid major
Posterior deltoid
Biceps brachii

Trapezius

Teres major

Latissimus
dorsi

Execution

1. Sit on a seated low-row machine with cables and pulleys, brace yourself, and grasp the handles to initiate the exercise movement.

2. Keeping your back straight and perpendicular to the floor, reach forward with the weighted handles to an extended arm position. Notice the stretching of your latissimus dorsi, rhomboids, and posterior deltoid.

3. Pull the handles into your lower chest, engaging the latissimus dorsi while squeezing your shoulder blades together. Remember to keep your spine erect.

4. Extend back to the starting position, and repeat for the required number of repetitions.

Muscles Involved

Primary: Latissimus dorsi

Secondary: Trapezius, rhomboid major, rhomboid minor, teres major, posterior deltoid, biceps brachii

Triathlon Focus

Again this upper-back exercise develops key muscle groups used in open-water swimming and is essential for the serious triathlete to perform in training. It does a particularly outstanding job of strengthening the scapular stabilizers, which leads to a strong base of support for the entire shoulder girdle.

Although the movement itself is not specific to freestyle swimming, the work done and the muscles targeted will help generate more force during the pulling phase of the stroke. The cyclist will experience greater control of the bike, especially when her hands are on the cow horns and she is pulling hard during steep and difficult climbing efforts.

Dumbbell Shrug

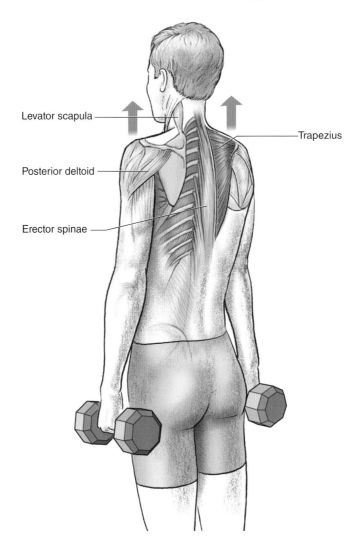

Levator scapula

Trapezius

Posterior deltoid

Erector spinae

Execution

1. Stand with your spine erect. Hold a dumbbell in each hand.
2. Pull your shoulders up to your ears (shrug them), keeping your arms straight.
3. Return to the starting position, and repeat for the required number of repetitions.

Muscles Involved

Primary: Trapezius

Secondary: Posterior deltoid, levator scapulae, erector spinae

Triathlon Focus

Although triathletes don't need huge trapezius muscles (or necks) like American football players do, it's still a good idea to perform shrugs in a strength training routine.

In cycling, the muscles targeted in this exercise will be particularly noticeable when the athlete is climbing out of the saddle during moderate to steep climbs as well as during intense sprint efforts.

The runner, especially the Ironman-distance triathlete who endures miles and miles of running in training and racing, will benefit from shrugs by strengthening the trapezius and surrounding muscle groups necessary to maintain proper upper-arm positioning for extended periods of time, when fatigue can negatively affect form and technique.

VARIATION

Barbell Shrug

This exercise can also be effectively performed by using a barbell in place of dumbbells. Hold the barbell in an overhand grip.

Barbell Pull-Up

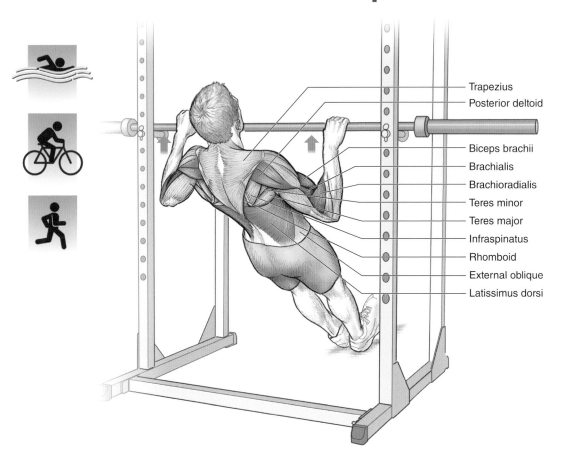

Trapezius
Posterior deltoid
Biceps brachii
Brachialis
Brachioradialis
Teres minor
Teres major
Infraspinatus
Rhomboid
External oblique
Latissimus dorsi

Execution

1. Use a Smith machine or other low bar set at approximately waist height.
2. Position your body under the bar. Grasp the bar in an overhand grip, hanging with your body straight and your arms fully extended. Your body should be at an approximately 45-degree angle to the floor.
3. Pull your chest up to the bar, attempting to touch the bar near your sternum.
4. Lower your body, and repeat for the required number of repetitions.

Muscles Involved

Primary: Latissimus dorsi, biceps brachii, brachialis, brachioradialis, posterior deltoid

Secondary: Rhomboid major, rhomboid minor, teres major, teres minor, infraspinatus, external oblique, trapezius

Triathlon Focus

This exercise targets many of the same muscle groups as the pull-up, with a stronger emphasis on the posterior deltoid. The key for successful execution is to keep the body straight throughout the movement. Most people find this exercise difficult to perform at first and should be patient, as results will eventually come.

The triathlete will benefit from this exercise in many ways, including greater back strength for improved swimming and enhanced stability and climbing leverage on the bike when standing. Runners will notice improved posture and less fatigue in the back muscles during long endurance runs.

Deadlift

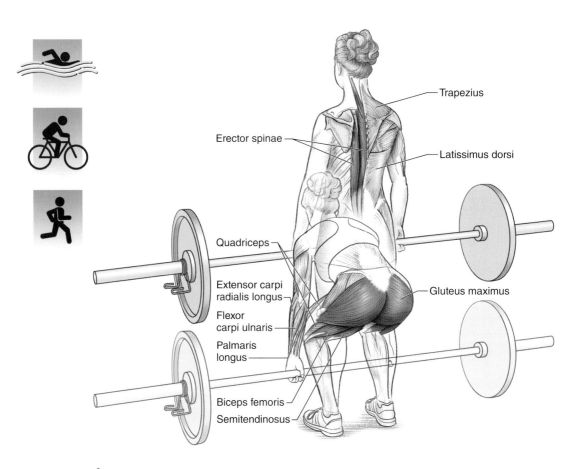

⚠ SAFETY TIP Take care to perform this exercise in the correct manner, including maintaining a straight back while looking up and forward throughout the range of motion.

Execution

1. Placing your feet about shoulder-width apart, bend at the knees and grasp the barbell with an overhand grip. Be sure the barbell is loaded with the appropriate weight.
2. With your back flat and spine straight, look ahead and keep your chin up.
3. Lift the weight off the floor as you rise to a full standing position, gently allowing the barbell to brush against your shins. Keep your back straight, and focus on activating the strong muscles of your quadriceps, buttocks, hamstrings, and low back.
4. Slowly lower the weight in the same fashion until it settles on the floor. Do not bounce the weight. Repeat for the required number of repetitions.

Muscles Involved

Primary: Erector spinae, gluteus maximus, hamstrings (biceps femoris, semitendinosus, semimembranosus)

Secondary: Trapezius, latissimus dorsi, quadriceps (rectus femoris, vastus lateralis, vastus medialis, vastus intermedius), forearms (extensor carpi radialis longus, flexor carpi ulnaris, palmaris longus)

Triathlon Focus

The deadlift is a great all-around exercise that elicits full-body strength gains because of the many large muscle groups engaged during the movement. In particular, this exercise targets the erector spinae, gluteus maximus, and hamstrings. Many strength coaches also applaud the deadlift movement as a way to boost the production of muscle-building hormones.

Triathletes will benefit from performing the deadlift by developing greater lower-body, core, and back strength and endurance, especially during longer-distance race events. It is not uncommon for long-course triathletes to experience issues with low-back fatigue caused by bending over on the bike and pounding the pavement during long runs. Furthermore, long-distance open-water swimming can cause a tremendous amount of low-back fatigue if the athlete is not properly conditioned. A regular schedule of deadlift training will minimize, if not alleviate, many of these issues.

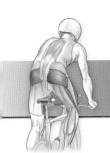

Power and speed are two qualities every triathlete dreams about. Both beginners and highly competitive athletes want to know the secret. The unfortunate truth is there is no secret other than hard work.

As important as upper-extremity strength and core stability are with respect to triathlon training and racing, the lower extremities provide the biggest bang for the buck by providing the largest propulsive force for making us fast. Everyone knows the stronger the engine, the faster we go.

Our lower extremities were designed specifically for efficient bipedal gait. How this efficiency translates to swimming, biking, and running is yet to be determined. What is known is that to improve athletic performance, you must maximize muscular strength, defined as force production; increase power, defined as the amount of force produced over a specific distance; and improve endurance, defined as the length of time the muscles can sustain that power. Training can help achieve these goals.

Strength and power can be developed by isolated strength training, such as a leg extension to isolate the quadriceps, and sport-specific strength training, such as a lunge that uses multiple muscles. The question is whether or not the methods differ in their effects on performance. The answer is not so simple except to say that muscles respond to stress or resistance training by enlarging each muscle fiber regardless of the specific exercise. We don't make more muscle fibers, they just get bigger. Resistance created by lifting a static weight from the ground or resistance felt from pushing a big gear up a hill stresses each muscle or group of muscles proportionately to its use and will produce strength and power gains if done correctly.

Genetics plays a large role in determining those who can sprint and those who can run long distances. Muscle fibers can be divided into Type I (fast twitch) and Type II (slow twitch). Fast-twitch fibers are for quick contractions and use anaerobic energy. Slow-twitch fibers are for endurance activities and use aerobic energy (see chapter 2). Each person has a genetically determined ratio of each type. Unfortunately we cannot change this ratio, but we can train each fiber type with both isolated strength training and sport-specific exercises.

An advantage of sport-specific strength training is that it can help maintain muscular symmetry and lower-extremity biomechanics. This is an essential concept in injury prevention. Fatigue and weakness of the lower-extremity muscles can cause muscular imbalances that contribute to poor running and biking form and poor swimming body position. Injury may result from abnormal stress to the other tissues of the lower extremities but also of the back and upper extremities as they compensate for the loss of body balance.

Anatomy of the Lower Extremities

The anatomy of the lower extremities includes the femur, the long bone of the thigh; the tibia and fibula of the lower leg; many bones of the foot and ankle; and the many muscles that cross each joint. These structures allow for efficient, stable gait. The lower extremities attach to the rest of the body, or axial skeleton, through the hip joint of the pelvis (figure 9.1). As we walk, run, or apply force to our legs, stress is transmitted to the pelvis and spine. The muscle contractions help deflect and dissipate these forces. Muscles not only provide force for motion but also can be thought of as dynamic shock absorbers. As discussed in chapter 8, the back and its S shape also help absorb the impact.

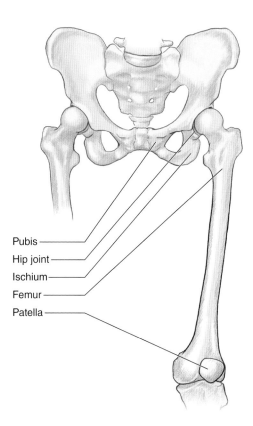

Pubis
Hip joint
Ischium
Femur
Patella

Figure 9.1 Bony structures of the upper leg.

The coordinated motions of the upper extremities, lower extremities, and pelvis create a gait cycle. The gait cycle (figure 9.2) can be described as a stance phase, when one foot is on the ground, and a swing phase, when the opposite foot is off the ground, swinging forward in preparation for foot planting. When walking, there is always one foot on the ground at all times in the stance phase. In running, though, at some point both feet are in the air at the same time. At foot impact in this unsupported position, approximately three times one's body weight is transmitted to the lower extremity.

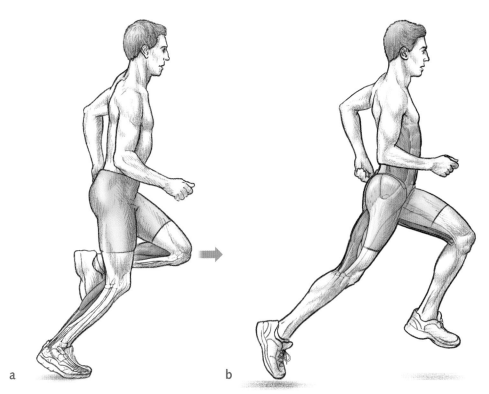

Figure 9.2 The gait cycle: *(a)* stance phase; *(b)* swing phase.

Normal, healthy anatomy allows for a smooth and economical gait cycle and subsequent running form. Of all three triathlon activities, running places the highest impact load on the skeleton. Biking and swimming, which are lower impact by nature, place other biomechanical demands on the lower extremities because of their somewhat unnatural motions. Over time, weight-bearing joints such as the hip and knee can be exposed to significant forces during impact activities. The potential risk for injury and subsequent development of arthritis is of utmost concern. At this point, however, there is a lack of scientific evidence that participation in endurance activities predisposes an athlete to arthritis. Continue with your training and racing without the fear of long-term injury and degeneration.

The muscles of the lower extremities (figure 9.3) can be broken down into groups based on their actions at each joint, including the hip, knee, foot, and ankle. Motions that occur include flexion, extension, abduction, adduction, rotation, and sometimes a combination to create inversion and eversion at the ankle. Many individual muscles create a single motion about a joint, but a few control motion at two joints.

Flexion at the hip, lifting the thigh up, is done by a group of muscles collectively known as the iliopsoas (psoas major, psoas minor, and iliacus). They originate from the deep aspect of the lower anterior spine and pelvis. They attach to a bony prominence on the upper part of the femur called the lesser trochanter. These muscles control a single motion about the hip.

Secondary movers of the hip are from the anterior compartment of the thigh, including the rectus femoris and sartorius. They originate on the pelvis and cross both hip and

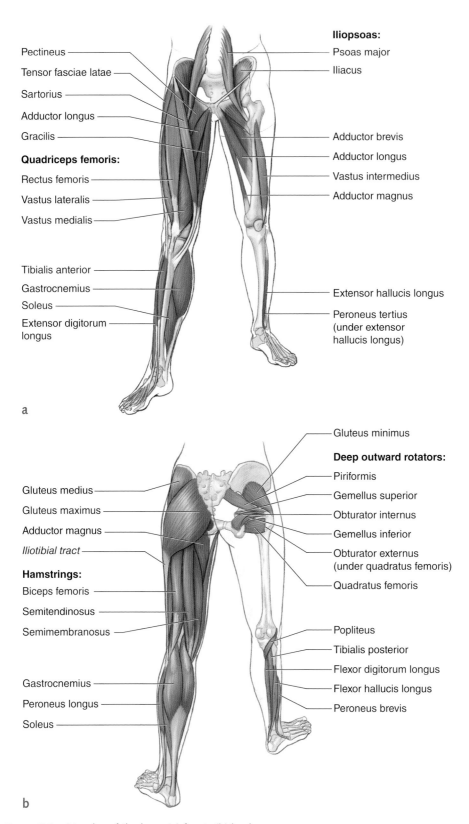

Pectineus

Tensor fasciae latae

Sartorius

Adductor longus

Gracilis

Quadriceps femoris:

Rectus femoris

Vastus lateralis

Vastus medialis

Tibialis anterior

Gastrocnemius

Soleus

Extensor digitorum
longus

Iliopsoas:

Psoas major

Iliacus

Adductor brevis

Adductor longus

Vastus intermedius

Adductor magnus

Extensor hallucis longus

Peroneus tertius
(under extensor
hallucis longus)

a

Gluteus minimus

Deep outward rotators:

Piriformis

Gemellus superior

Obturator internus

Gemellus inferior

Obturator externus
(under quadratus femoris)

Quadratus femoris

Gluteus medius

Gluteus maximus

Adductor magnus

Iliotibial tract

Hamstrings:

Biceps femoris

Semitendinosus

Semimembranosus

Gastrocnemius

Peroneus longus

Soleus

Popliteus

Tibialis posterior

Flexor digitorum longus

Flexor hallucis longus

Peroneus brevis

b

Figure 9.3 Muscles of the legs: *(a)* front; *(b)* back.

knee joints, inserting into the patella and proximal tibia, respectively. The rectus femoris facilitates hip flexion and knee extension, or straightening. The sartorius also aids in hip flexion but also helps knee flexion, or bending. This concept of muscles acting across two joints is essential when understanding how sport-specific exercises are an important aspect of training, which is discussed in chapter 10.

Hip extension, or pushing the thigh back, is controlled by the gluteus maximus. The gluteus maximus is the largest of the gluteal muscles and a large portion of the shape and appearance of the buttocks. From an evolutionary standpoint, the large size of the gluteus maximus is characteristic of an erect stance and upright gait as it helps maintain posture and regain erect position after bending over.

Hip abduction, or lifting the leg away from the midline of the body, is essentially controlled by the gluteus medius and gluteus minimus. These two muscles originate from the iliac wing of the pelvis and insert into the bony prominence of the femur, the greater trochanter. This is the bone you feel on the side of your hip. These muscles, along with the other abductor (tensor fasciae latae, which runs from the crest of the iliac wing and inserts along the outside of the proximal tibia as the iliotibial band), control hip and pelvis motion through the gait cycle. In a single-leg stance, the body's center of gravity is medial, or more midline, to the hip and leg on the standing side.

Hip abduction on the weight-bearing leg counteracts the body weight to keep the body from falling over the leg in the swing phase of the gait. In this situation, the abductors are pelvic stabilizers that hold the pelvis level and create a stable mechanical axis. This stable platform, with the help of good core control, maintains proper knee and foot biomechanics and helps prevent injury.

Hip adduction, pulling the leg toward the midline, is controlled primarily by the pectineus, gracilis, adductor brevis, adductor longus, and adductor magnus. Each muscle has secondary functions as a hip flexor and hip rotator. The clinical significance of this group relates to what we refer to as a groin strain. Injury to the adductor muscles can cause pain and tightness about the hip. Beware that other structures in this region can cause similar symptoms. Groin pain can also be caused by an injury to the bones of the hip, including a stress fracture; an injury or tear of the labrum (the fibrous ring that surrounds the hip); or deterioration of the joint cartilage surface, described as arthritis.

Hip external rotation—pointing the toes and knee out—occurs primarily through the posterior hip rotators including the piriformis, obturator muscles, gemelli, and quadratus femoris. Internal rotation is performed by the gluteus medius and gluteus minimus in conjunction with the adductors.

The bones that make up the knee are the distal femur; upper tibia, called the tibial plateau; fibula; and the patella, or kneecap. Articular cartilage of the knee provides a low-friction surface between the femur and tibia (tibiofemoral articulation) and the patella and femur (patellofemoral joint). The function of the patella and its articulation with the femur provides a mechanical fulcrum that helps generate quadriceps forces. Running and jumping facilitated by quadriceps contraction can produce forces three to five times body weight in the patellofemoral joint.

Knee stability is maintained by a set of four ligaments (figure 9.4). The medial and lateral collateral ligaments provide side-to-side stability. The anterior and posterior cruciate ligaments provide front-to-back stability. The anterior cruciate ligament, or ACL, also provides rotatory stability to the knee and is one of the most frequently injured knee ligaments during pivoting sport activities.

Knee extension, or straightening, is controlled through the anterior thigh muscles of the quadriceps femoris. Four muscles make up the quadriceps femoris, including the rectus femoris, which is surrounded by the vastus intermedius, vastus medialis, and vastus lateralis. The rectus femoris originates at the pelvis, whereas the vasti originate from the proximal femur. Together they unite at the knee and form a common tendon, the quadriceps tendon, and a layer of tissue surrounding the patella called the retinaculum. The patellar tendon attaches the patella to the tibia. The retinaculum, quadriceps muscle, quadriceps tendon, patella, and patellar tendon together make up the extensor mechanism of the knee. Its main function is to straighten the knee.

The posterior thigh and knee muscles, collectively referred to as the hamstrings, include the biceps femoris, semitendinosus, and semimembranosus. The biceps femoris has two points of origin, one from a bony prominence of the pelvis, the ischial tuberosity, the bone you sit on, and the other from the back of the shaft of the femur. Both heads combine at the knee and form a common tendon that inserts into the head of the fibula on the lateral aspect of the knee. The primary function of the biceps femoris is to flex, or bend, the knee, but it also acts as a knee lateral rotator. The semitendinosus and semimembranosus, referred to as the medial hamstrings, originate from the pelvis and insert along the medial, or inside, aspect of the tibia. Because the muscles cross two joints, they extend the hip, flex the knee, and medially rotate the leg. These medial hamstrings along with the sartorius and gracilis form the pes anserine tendons. They insert along the upper medial border of the proximal tibia. When working together, they function as knee and hip flexors as well as external rotators of the hip and thigh. This motion pattern is essential when walking to help clear the foot as the walker passes from the stance to the swing phase of the gait.

The ankle, which is made up of the distal tibia, distal fibula, and talus (figure 9.5), allows for dorsiflexion (bringing the ankle up) and (plantar flexion) pointing the ankle down. The bones below the talus, including the calcaneus (heel bone) and the midfoot bones, allow for complex motions that are essential for normal gait. Inversion is defined as plantar flexion and internal rotation of the ankle and foot, and eversion is dorsiflexion and external rotation. Without this series of motions, we would have a very difficult time accommodating uneven surfaces.

Ankle stability is provided by a strong ligament system as well as a contribution from the lateral leg muscles the peroneus longus and peroneus brevis, which act as dynamic ankle stabilizers. The lateral ligaments of the ankle, including the anterior talofibular and calcaneofibular ligaments, resist inversion forces placed on the ankle.

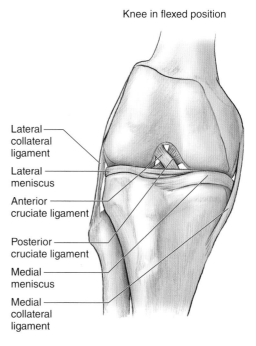

Knee in flexed position

Lateral collateral ligament

Lateral meniscus

Anterior cruciate ligament

Posterior cruciate ligament

Medial meniscus

Medial collateral ligament

Figure 9.4   Knee ligaments and tissues.

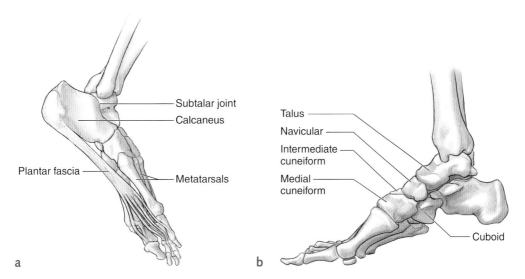

Figure 9.5 Bones and tissues of the foot: *(a)* underside showing the plantar fascia; *(b)* medial side.

When someone refers to rolling an ankle, which is the most common mechanism of injury, these ligaments are frequently torn.

The deltoid ligament on the medial aspect of the ankle connects the distal tibia, or medial malleolus, to the calcaneus and talus. In more severe sprains, this ligament becomes injured. The last set of strong ankle-stabilizing ligaments connects the distal fibula to the tibia and is referred to as the tib-fib ligaments. Injury to these ligaments from rotational forces is called a high ankle sprain, as the ligaments are located above the joint level. This injury often takes longer than other sprains to heal.

Muscles of the calf (figure 9.6) control ankle motion. The gastrocnemius, which arises from the distal femur, and the soleus, which originates on the tibia, join near the ankle to form the Achilles tendon, which attaches to the calcaneus, or heel bone. They are responsible for plantar flexion and are the main source of push-off strength. Although the Achilles is the largest and strongest tendon in the body, it is also the site of a spectrum of injuries including inflammation and rupture.

The anterior muscles of the calf, including the tibialis anterior, extensor hallucis longus, and extensor digitorum, produce dorsiflexion of the foot. This essential motion is responsible for clearing the foot as it goes through the swing phase of the gait from toe push-off to heel strike. Without this motion, the foot would drop and the toes would drag as the foot swings forward. An injury to the peroneal nerve that innervates this muscle group can cause this problem. This is not a common injury but is sometimes a complication of hip replacement surgery.

The last group of muscles is the peroneals, the peroneus longus and peroneus brevis. They originate from the fibula and run down the lateral side of the ankle around the fibula and insert along the foot and toes. Their main function is to produce eversion of the ankle. Functionally this motion creates dynamic ankle stability. After an ankle sprain and subsequent

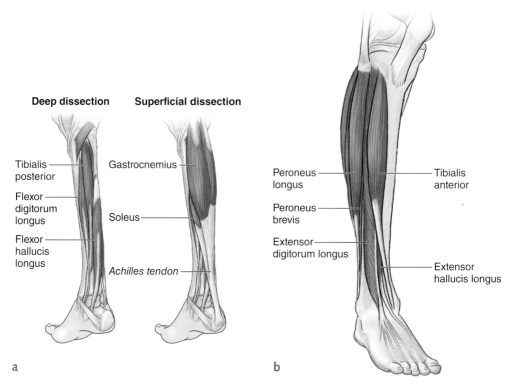

Figure 9.6   Muscles of the lower leg and foot: *(a)* back; *(b)* front.

healing of the ligaments, these muscles require equal attention to rehabilitation to restore complete functional healing.

The foot and ankle are made up of 26 bones; more than 30 joints; and more than 100 muscles, tendons, and ligaments. The extrinsic muscles, those that originate in the lower leg and insert into the foot, have been described. The intrinsic group of muscles of the foot are small and strong and help produce a smooth gait pattern.

Exercises for the Legs

The triathlete needs to be strategic when it comes to training the legs to build strength. Considerations regarding the time in the annual training season relative to race season and training volumes for cycling and running, among other factors, will influence the amount and quality of resistance training for the legs. The main area of concern is always adequate recovery and maximizing gains from sport-specific training. It's important to remember that brute strength and power rarely translate to running a faster 10K or riding faster over the course of 112 miles. Sport specificity is a key training principle all endurance athletes must stick to, using strength training as a supplement to benefit performance and reduce the risk of injury.

As with other areas of strength training, the legs should be trained to develop strength and muscular endurance. Therefore, consider performing two to four sets of 10 to 15 repetitions for selected exercises in your routine, with about 1 to 2 minutes of rest between each set.

The following exercises are a combination of isolated and sport-specific multijoint movements. Perform them only after an adequate warm-up. This might include 10 to 15 minutes of easy aerobic exercise followed by some stretching, which could include dynamic as well as gentle static stretches. Perform leg strength training two or three times per week during preseason training and one or two times a week during the season for maintenance and injury prevention.

Barbell Squat

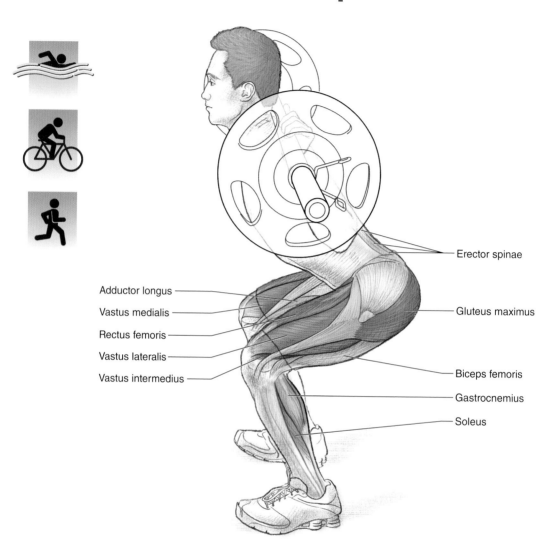

Erector spinae

Adductor longus

Vastus medialis

Rectus femoris

Vastus lateralis

Vastus intermedius

Gluteus maximus

Biceps femoris

Gastrocnemius

Soleus

⚠ **SAFETY TIP** Good form is crucial. Maintain a flat back throughout the exercise, and never bounce at the bottom of the movement. Elevate your heels slightly with a board, if necessary, and warm up thoroughly before starting this exercise.

Execution

1. Place a weighted barbell on your upper shoulders, and stand with your feet about the same distance apart (or slightly wider) as when you ride your bike and are clipped into your pedals.
2. Keeping a straight back, bend down to a squat position until your upper thighs are almost parallel to the floor.

3. Maintaining a straight back and engaged core, activate the muscles in the buttocks and the legs to return to the starting position. Repeat for the required number of repetitions.

Muscles Involved

Primary: Gluteus maximus, quadriceps (rectus femoris, vastus lateralis, vastus medialis, vastus intermedius)

Secondary: Erector spinae, hamstrings (biceps femoris, semitendinosus, semimembranosus), gastrocnemius, soleus, hip adductors

Triathlon Focus

Long touted as the best overall lower-body exercise for strength development, the traditional barbell squat still reigns supreme when it comes to effectiveness. A multijoint movement that engages key muscles in the legs, buttocks, hips, and core, it's hard to find a lower-body exercise that offers more of a bang for the buck than the squat.

For the triathlon cyclist, stronger quadriceps developed through this movement will help generate more power with less fatigue on each pedal stroke, in particular during the powerful downstroke as the leg passes the crank through the 90-degree position.

The swimmer will notice a more powerful push off the wall during practices in the pool, as well as more propulsion from the kick. The triathlon runner will be able to drive uphill with more spring in her legs and with more force, even when fatigued coming off a hard bike effort.

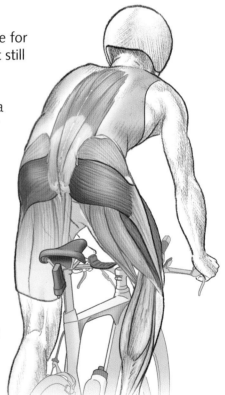

VARIATION

Dumbbell Squat

This exercise is performed in a similar fashion to the barbell squat but with dumbbells instead. Simply grasp two evenly weighted dumbbells, and hold them down at your sides while performing the squat movement with a flat back.

Lunge

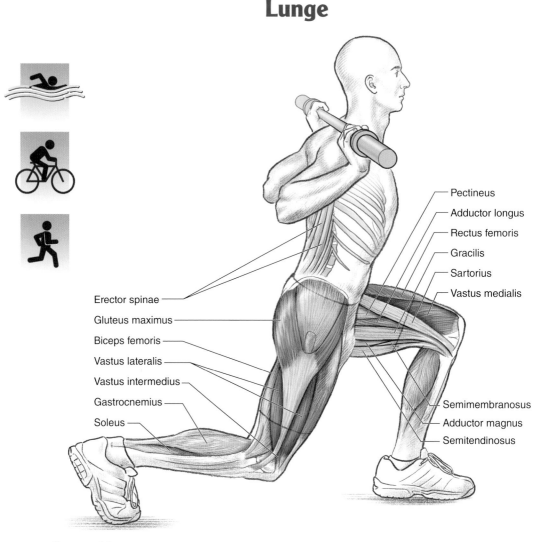

Pectineus
Adductor longus
Rectus femoris
Gracilis
Sartorius
Vastus medialis

Erector spinae
Gluteus maximus
Biceps femoris
Vastus lateralis
Vastus intermedius
Gastrocnemius
Soleus

Semimembranosus
Adductor magnus
Semitendinosus

Execution

1. Stand with your feet about shoulder-width apart. If you are using added resistance, place a barbell comfortably and evenly on your shoulders, or hold a dumbbell of the same weight in each hand.

2. Keeping your back straight with your head up and looking forward, gently step forward (lunge) until your upper leg is parallel to the ground, your bent knee forming a 90-degree angle with the floor. The knee of your trailing leg should almost touch the floor. Maintain your posture throughout the movement.

3. After a brief pause, explosively activate the muscles in the quadriceps of the forward leg while maintaining your balance and posture as you return to the starting position.

4. Repeat this action with the opposite foot leading. Repeat for the required number of repetitions.

Muscles Involved

Primary: Gluteus maximus, quadriceps (rectus femoris, vastus lateralis, vastus medialis, vastus intermedius)

Secondary: Erector spinae, hamstrings (biceps femoris, semitendinosus, semimembranosus), gastrocnemius, soleus, hip adductors

Triathlon Focus

Ask any elite triathlete which single lower-body strength training exercise plays a key role in his success and he'll likely mention the lunge. Targeting the powerful muscles of the quadriceps (rectus femoris, vastus lateralis, vastus medialis, vastus intermedius), hamstrings (biceps femoris, semitendinosus, semimembranosus), and gluteus maximus, this simple yet effective exercise offers the athlete an effective means of building strength and power for faster cycling and running.

The lunge, especially the walking lunge, is a multipurpose lower-body exercise that works not only to increase a triathlete's ability to turn a larger gear on the bike and to charge uphill faster on the run but also functions as a dynamic warm-up and stretching movement recommended before running workouts. In addition, proper execution of the movement enhances proprioception and balance.

Be cautious when performing the lunge, whether using barbells or dumbbells or using only body weight. Proper form dictates that you keep your back straight and that your knee stays behind your toe when stepping out so as not to overstress the patellar tendon.

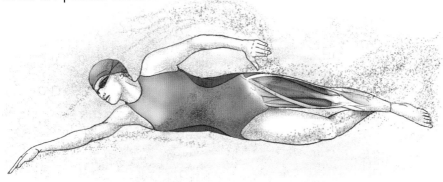

VARIATION

Walking Lunge

The walking lunge is a fantastic dynamic warm-up exercise when done without additional weights. Simply do the lunge movement and repeat with the opposite leg as you walk for the required number of repetitions. Additional weights can be added to increase the intensity of this movement.

Single-Leg Squat

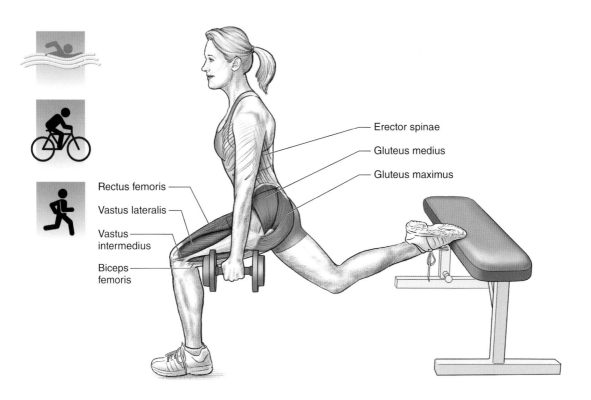

Erector spinae

Gluteus medius

Gluteus maximus

Rectus femoris

Vastus lateralis

Vastus intermedius

Biceps femoris

⚠ **SAFETY TIP** Like double-leg squats, never bounce at the bottom of the movement as this places undue stress on the knee.

Execution

1. Perform this movement with body weight only, or hold a dumbbell in each hand.

2. Stand 2 to 3 feet (.6 to .9 m) in front of a weight bench or other solid support. Reach back with the nonworking leg, placing it on the bench, and find a balanced position.

3. Bend your front knee to lower your body until your thigh is parallel to the ground, activating the muscles of the hips, buttocks, and quadriceps.

4. Straighten your front leg to return to the starting position, and repeat for the required number of repetitions. Switch legs and repeat.

Muscles Involved

Primary: Quadriceps (rectus femoris, vastus medialis, vastus lateralis, vastus intermedius), gluteus maximus, gluteus medius

Secondary: Erector spinae, biceps femoris, adductor longus, adductor brevis, transversus abdominis, internal oblique, external oblique

Triathlon Focus

The single-leg squat offers many of the same muscle development benefits of the double-leg squat but with the ability to isolate one leg at a time and focus more on weaknesses and balance.

The broad range of muscles engaged by this exercise makes it ideal for the triathlete, in particular for the sports of cycling and running. The cyclist will improve her ability to produce power throughout the pedaling stroke. The runner will gain greater propulsion, especially when running uphill. Overall, single-leg squats should be a key exercise in a lower-body strength training routine.

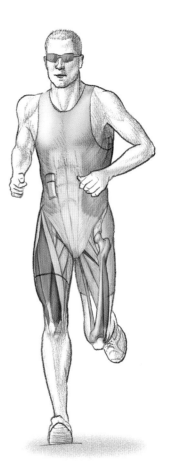

Dumbbell Step-Up

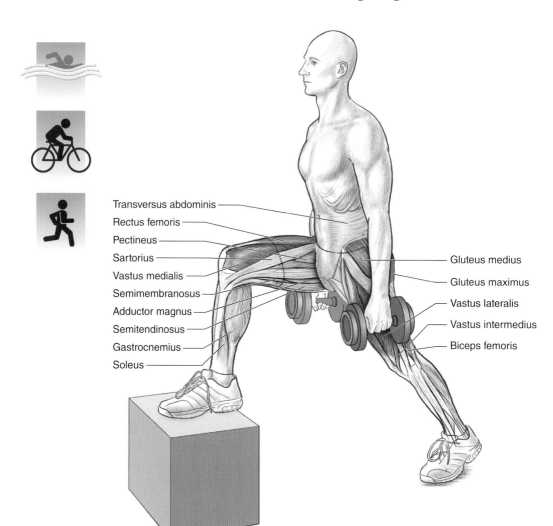

Transversus abdominis
Rectus femoris
Pectineus
Sartorius
Vastus medialis
Semimembranosus
Adductor magnus
Semitendinosus
Gastrocnemius
Soleus

Gluteus medius
Gluteus maximus
Vastus lateralis
Vastus intermedius
Biceps femoris

Execution

1. Use a plyometric or other sturdy box approximately the height of your knee, and stand facing it with a dumbbell in each hand.
2. Step onto the box with the exercising leg, pressing up onto the box until standing on it with both feet.
3. Return to the starting position. Perform the same stepping movement with the opposite leg. Repeat for the required number of repetitions.

Muscles Involved

Primary: Quadriceps (rectus femoris, vastus medialis, vastus intermedius, vastus lateralis), psoas major, gluteus maximus, gluteus medius

Secondary: Hamstrings (biceps femoris, semitendinosus, semimembranosus), adductor magnus, adductor brevis, pectineus, sartorius, gastrocnemius, soleus, transversus abdominis

Triathlon Focus

This is another great exercise for targeting the lower-body muscles as well as increasing balance and stability. Performing this exercise in a slow and controlled manner will further increase its effectiveness.

The triathlete who incorporates this exercise into his strength training routine will notice improved power output on the bike, a stronger and more propulsive kick in the swim, and more energetic bounding uphill on the run. This exercise will also strengthen connective tissues, helping to prevent injury. Increase the intensity of this exercise by either adding more weight or raising the height of the step-up box.

Stability Ball Hamstring Curl

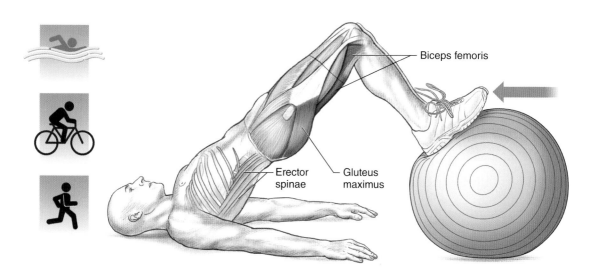

Biceps femoris

Erector spinae

Gluteus maximus

Execution

1. Using a medium-diameter stability ball, lie on your back with the ball under your heels.
2. Engaging your core, gently lift your hips toward the ceiling so that your body is straight.
3. Pull your heels toward your buttocks until the knee joints form about a 90-degree angle.
4. Straighten your legs back to the starting position, keeping your body straight and supported on the ground with your upper back and on the ball with your heels.

Muscles Involved

Primary: Gluteus maximus, hamstrings (biceps femoris, semitendinosus, semimembranosus)

Secondary: Erector spinae

Triathlon Focus

This exercise is convenient and effective for the busy triathlete who might not have the time to go to the gym to use strength equipment that targets and isolates the hamstrings and gluteus. In addition, it targets key muscles in the legs as well as those in the core for added bang for your buck.

The stability ball hamstring curl will help strengthen muscles used in cycling, particularly when climbing or riding into a headwind when pulling up on the pedals is important. Runners will benefit from having stronger hamstrings and glutes, especially when running into a stiff headwind or when attacking a hill where these key muscle groups are required to perform at an optimal level.

Note that a strong core is required to perform this exercise properly. Be certain to read the section on core strengthening exercises in this book.

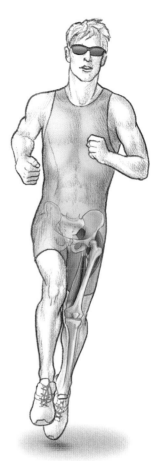

VARIATION

Single-Leg Stability Ball Hamstring Curl

The variation of a double-leg curl is the single-leg curl. This movement requires greater balance and core stability. To perform this variation, simply use one leg for the required number of repetitions, keeping the opposite leg extended throughout the movement. Repeat with the other leg.

Leg Curl

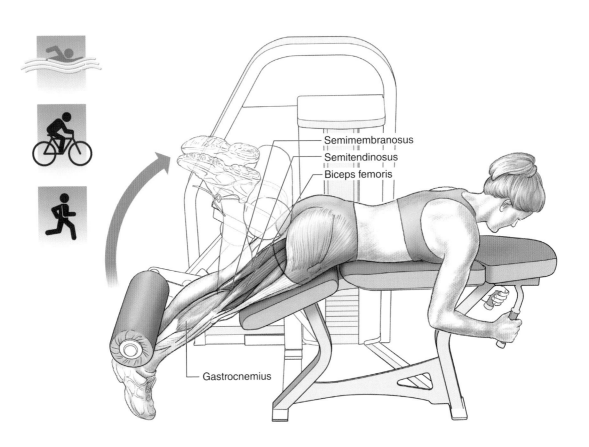

Semimembranosus
Semitendinosus
Biceps femoris

Gastrocnemius

Execution

1. Lying facedown on a hamstring curl machine, position your heels underneath the pads.
2. Focus on engaging the hamstring muscles as you curl the weight toward your buttocks.
3. Slowly return the weight to the starting position, and repeat for the required number of repetitions.

Muscles Involved

Primary: Hamstrings (biceps femoris, semitendinosus, semimembranosus)

Secondary: Gastrocnemius

Triathlon Focus

Strong hamstrings are important for balancing out the possible disproportionate strength of the quadriceps on the front of the thigh and aiding in the prevention of injury. This exercise isolates the hamstrings most effectively.

Whether cycling or running, the triathlete engages the hamstrings constantly when turning the cranks or running uphill. Strong hamstrings help add power and speed necessary to perform at the highest level.

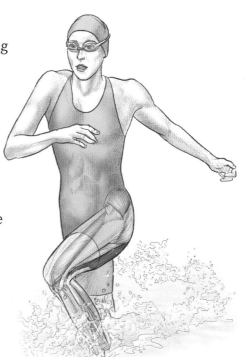

Leg Extension

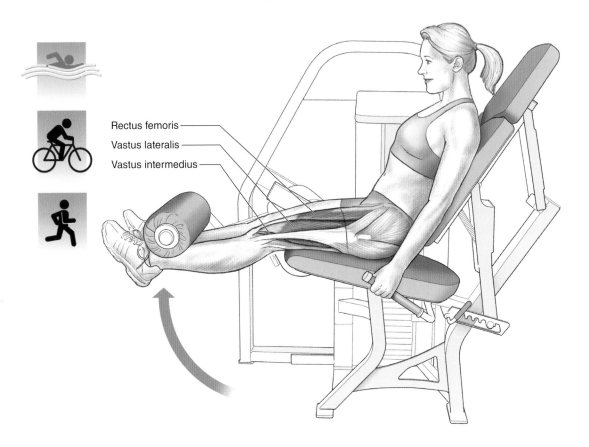

Rectus femoris
Vastus lateralis
Vastus intermedius

Execution

1. While sitting comfortably on a leg extension machine, place your feet underneath the pads.
2. Slowly extend your legs, activating the front of the thigh, until your legs are straight.
3. Slowly return the weight to the starting position, and repeat for the required number of repetitions.

Muscles Involved

Primary: Quadriceps (rectus femoris, vastus lateralis, vastus intermedius, vastus medialis)

Triathlon Focus

This exercise isolates the quadriceps muscle group and is valuable for strengthening muscles that surround and support the knee, which triathletes commonly injure when cycling or running. In addition, by isolating the quadriceps muscles, leg extensions enhance cycling and running power output and possibly correct strength imbalances between the muscles in the front and back of the leg.

The key to this exercise is performing it slowly and methodically, with a reasonable resistance. Do not cheat by throwing the weight up or allowing it to return to the starting position rapidly, without resisting.

Machine Adduction

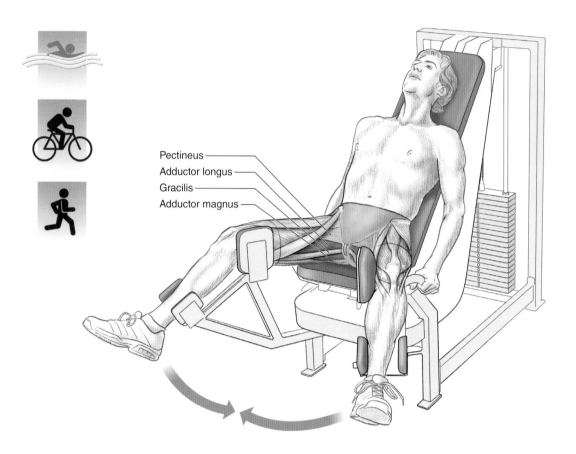

Pectineus
Adductor longus
Gracilis
Adductor magnus

Execution

1. Sit on an adduction machine with your legs spread.
2. Close your legs together until the pads touch lightly.
3. Slowly reopen your legs to the starting position. Repeat for the required number of repetitions.

Muscles Involved

Primary: Adductor magnus, adductor longus

Secondary: Gracilis, pectineus, lower gluteus maximus

Triathlon Focus

Although this exercise doesn't simulate a movement pattern specific to swimming, cycling, or running, it's still an important supplemental exercise that develops the supporting muscle groups, helping to boost overall performance and prevent injuries caused by muscle imbalances.

The cyclist and the runner will benefit by having strong adductor muscles, primarily in regard to maintaining good form as fatigue starts to set in. In particular for the cyclist, the legs will spin the pedals more smoothly and with grace and control. Runners will be more likely to maintain a balanced and efficient gait and foot-strike frequency count.

Cable or Elastic Band Hip Adduction

Use a low cable or an elastic band. While standing, perform the same movement and isolate the muscles responsible for adduction.

Machine Abduction

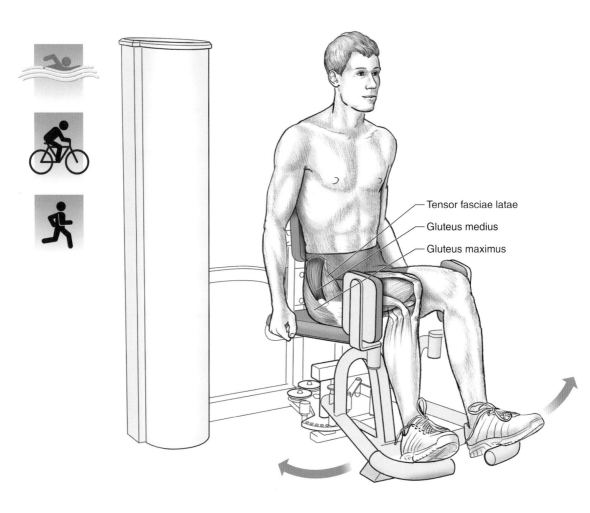

Tensor fasciae latae

Gluteus medius

Gluteus maximus

Execution

1. Sit comfortably in the abduction machine with the outsides of your quadriceps pressed against the pads.
2. Open your legs against the resistance of the machine.
3. Slowly return to the starting position. Repeat for the required number of repetitions.

Muscles Involved

Primary: Gluteus medius, gluteus minimus

Secondary: Gluteus maximus, piriformis, obturator externus, tensor fasciae latae

Triathlon Focus

Hip abduction exercises target another group of muscles responsible for stabilizing key movement patterns in both cycling and running, especially as fatigue begins to settle in during long or intense workouts or races.

Cyclists will increase their ability to smoothly deliver power throughout the entire pedal stroke. Runners will be able to better maintain a spring in their step in the late stages of a run.

VARIATION

Cable or Elastic Band Hip Abduction

Stand with the working leg attached to a low-pulley ankle apparatus, or use an elastic band. Perform the same basic movement pattern as with the machine, alternating legs.

Cable Kickback

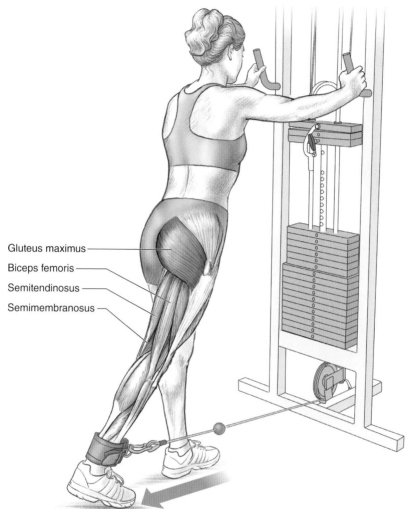

Gluteus maximus
Biceps femoris
Semitendinosus
Semimembranosus

Execution

1. Using a low-pulley machine, attach the ankle strap and face the machine.
2. Bracing yourself with your hands against the machine, move your straight working leg back, engaging the gluteus maximus and the hamstrings.
3. Return slowly to the starting position. Repeat for the required number of repetitions.

Muscles Involved

Primary: Gluteus maximus

Secondary: Hamstrings (biceps femoris, semitendinosus, semimembranosus)

Triathlon Focus

The gluteus maximus is a strong muscle that is engaged constantly during triathlon training and racing. Many complex exercises engage this muscle, but few isolate it as effectively as the cable kickback.

The gluteus maximus is a dominant source of power generation in cycling, especially during the initial phase of the downstroke when riding a triathlon bike. And runners will be able to generate more velocity with stronger glutes when driving up a steep hill and really digging in.

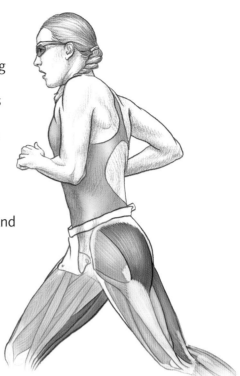

VARIATION

Stability Ball Hip Extension

Lie on your back with both legs on a stability ball; for added difficulty, work one leg at a time as shown in the illustration. Straighten your body at the hips, engaging the glutes to raise your hips.

Wall Stability-Ball Squat

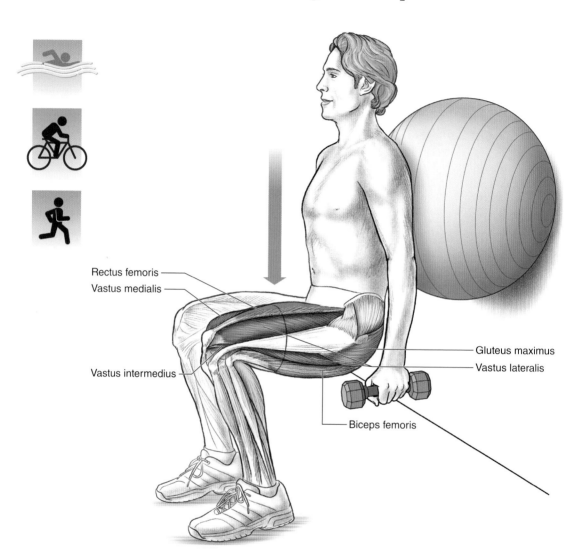

Rectus femoris

Vastus medialis

Vastus intermedius

Gluteus maximus

Vastus lateralis

Biceps femoris

Execution

1. From a standing position with your back to a wall and your heels about 3 feet (.9 m) from the wall, place a stability ball between your lower or middle back and the wall. If you like, add weight by holding a dumbbell in each hand.

2. While pressing back against the ball and maintaining your balance, lower your body to a sitting position, with your legs forming 90-degree angles.

3. Stand up and repeat for the required number of repetitions.

Muscles Involved

Primary: Quadriceps (rectus femoris, vastus lateralis, vastus medialis, vastus intermedius), gluteus maximus

Secondary: Hamstrings (biceps femoris, semitendinosus, semimembranosus), hip adductors

Triathlon Focus

The wall stability-ball squat targets many of the same muscle groups as the regular squat but with the added benefit of engaging the core and developing a sense of balance.

Strong legs developed through resistance movements such as this will increase power output for both the bike and the run as well as for the crucial transition from one discipline to the next in the sport of triathlon.

Another benefit to performing exercises such as this is time efficiency, as you'll be developing the components of core stability and leg strength and endurance all in one simple and very effective exercise.

Single-Leg Heel Raise With Dumbbells

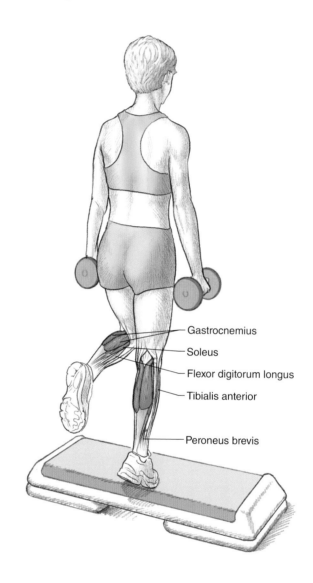

Gastrocnemius

Soleus

Flexor digitorum longus

Tibialis anterior

Peroneus brevis

Execution

1. Stand on a stable platform 3 to 5 inches (7.5 to 12.5 cm) high on the ball of one foot (the exercising leg). Hold appropriately weighted dumbbells in each hand or no weight, depending on your fitness level. For many athletes, the weight should be considered challenging to complete the desired number of repetitions.

2. Lower your heel toward the ground (dorsiflexion) until you feel a slight stretch in the calf muscles and surrounding region.

3. Slowly extend up (plantar flexion), engaging the muscles of the calf with your knee slightly flexed.

4. Again lower slowly and repeat for the required number of repetitions. Switch legs.

Muscles Involved

Primary: Gastrocnemius, soleus

Secondary: Tibialis anterior, peroneus brevis, flexor digitorum longus

Triathlon Focus

Effective for both injury prevention and performance, this is an important lower-leg isolation exercise for the triathlete that can both prevent injury and enhance cycling and running performance.

In both cycling and running, the lower leg is crucial for delivering power or propulsion. Inadequately strengthened muscles in this area will diminish performance potential as well as increase your risk of injury, most commonly to the Achilles tendon.

WHOLE-BODY TRAINING

Over the last few chapters we have outlined a series of exercises intended to strengthen specific groups of muscles necessary for triathlon participation. In reality, movement of the body doesn't come from isolated muscle contractions but involves a coordinated series of muscle interactions across multiple joints to create fluid motion. This whole-body involvement best describes what takes place during activities including swimming, biking, and running. An integral part of whole-body motion is the contribution of core stability to provide a stable platform for force generation and balance for efficient motion. The exercises in this chapter engage both core and multiple muscle groups that help develop sport-specific strength and improve performance.

The ability to perform an endurance activity depends not only on optimal muscular strength but also on its synergy with cardiorespiratory fitness. Cardiorespiratory fitness as defined by the body's ability to supply energy and sustain muscular activity is a function of both aerobic and anaerobic metabolism, discussed in chapter 2. Total-body exercises can increase strength but also improve cardiorespiratory fitness. As more muscle fibers and more groups of muscles are recruited, the heart and lungs need to supply more blood, oxygen, and glucose to these tissues to support activity. Although most weight training would be considered an anaerobic activity, aerobic fibers are still active during these exercises. It's important to note that many coaches prefer sport-specific strength development over other methods. Examples of this include swimming with hand paddles and drag suits; doing hill repeats on the bike while using a high resistance and low cadence; running stairs; running steep hill repeats; or using a resistance device, such as a parachute or an elastic cord held by a coach. Each of these serves to build strength that is specific to the movement pattern of each sport discipline and is beneficial to that sport specifically.

Resistance training with the use of weights or body weight develops strength. Generating motion and force across multiple joints along with performing multiple repetitions can also stress and improve the cardiorespiratory system. Secondary effects of this type of training also enhance the neuromuscular system. Nerve cells and the fibers that carry the signals from the brain through the spinal cord innervate the muscles and cause them to contract. A combination of electrical impulse and chemical release causes muscles to generate force and control voluntary muscle function. This transmission process is improved with these types of exercises. The end result can be an increased efficiency of motion, which can ultimately lead to decreased energy consumption. You feel this effect as you train and get into better shape. Workouts become easier, and you become stronger and faster. This process of early neuromuscular adaptation occurs with exercise but can be short lived. As the body gets used to each exercise, strength development and neuromuscular improvements can plateau. Periodization with training, as discussed in chapter 3, helps break the pattern of repetitive activity and allows for continued exercise improvement as well as helps prevent injuries.

Multijoint Exercises

The exercises described in this chapter are broken down into multijoint and plyometric activities. Multijoint exercises engage two or more groups of muscles that cross more than one joint. Motion about a joint often involves a pair of muscles that work synergistically.

This is referred to as an agonist and antagonist pair. An agonist is a muscle that causes specific movement, such as flexion, which is defined as bending the joint, or extension, straightening the joint. The antagonist muscle would cause the opposite motion. In the arm, as the biceps brachii contracts and bends the elbow, the triceps brachii relaxes and lets that motion occur. Similarly, when the elbow is straightened, or extended, the opposite occurs. This motion seems simple, but as you involve multiple joints and muscles, this basic contraction–relaxation mechanism becomes more complex.

To better understand this complex motion, you need to understand some basic concepts of muscle contraction and interaction during joint motion and concepts of muscle training. Muscles contract, or create tension, by staying the same length (isometric contraction), shortening (concentric contraction), or lengthening (eccentric contraction). Basic weight training uses the principles of open-chain and closed-chain exercises. More advanced techniques are available but often require specialized equipment. In open-chain exercises, force and motion are generated across a joint so the distal portion of the extremity—the hand or foot—is moving and free in space, such as a leg extension or biceps curl. A closed-chain exercise occurs when the distal portion of the foot or hand is fixed to the ground, such as a push-up or squat. A distinctive difference between open- and closed-chain exercises is the interplay between the agonists and antagonists. Throughout the motion of the lunge (closed-chain), there is a co-contraction of both agonists and antagonists. This reduces the force and stress on the joints, possibly preventing injury. Closed-chain exercises tend to offer increased functional benefits. Open-chain kinetic exercises isolate individual muscle groups and are best for muscle-specific strength gains. In training and racing, combinations of isometric, concentric, and eccentric contractions occur in all muscles, depending on the angle of the joints involved.

Plyometric Exercises

Plyometric exercises, a combination of eccentric and concentric explosive muscular contraction, are designed to produce fast, powerful movements. These exercises have been shown to improve sports performance, including power and speed. When a muscle is loaded or stretched and then forced to rapidly contract and produce motion, a plyometric activity is produced. This elastic recoil mechanism is demonstrated in the double-leg power jump. When concentrically contracting, muscles have a maximum potential of force generation. Eccentric loading of a muscle, referred to as preloading, creates a state in which force production can be increased past this point. The extent of stretch and the speed with which the muscle is loaded are two major factors that affect the extent of muscle force production. A shorter time between the eccentric and concentric contractions will also increase force production. When performing a double-leg power jump, the muscles of the lower extremity are stretched as you come down and squat. The transition to jumping and the subsequent muscular contraction allowing you to leave the ground completes the elastic recoil mechanism. Sensory nerve fibers within muscle are also activated and trained as the elastic recoil mechanism occurs. It is this type of exercise training that helps increase efficiency between brain and muscle.

Plyometric exercises have been shown to reduce lower-extremity injuries when combined with other exercises, including strength training, balance training, and stretching. There is a potential for increased injury, though, because of the large forces generated during these activities. Plyometric exercises should be performed only after an initial program of strength and flexibility training has been completed. A proper warm-up is essential before performing these exercises.

Exercises for the Entire Body

These exercises are considered to be effective for full-body training. Proper execution of each exercise in a strategically designed training program specific to the needs of the competitive triathlete is the key to success.

Because of the nature of full-body training, which tends to be very active and at times requires explosive output, a proper warm-up routine is highly recommended, including a series of dynamic stretches.

With regard to sets and repetitions, many coaches prescribe a time frame in which the athlete performs as many repetitions as possible with proper technique. This encourages the athlete to push his limits as well as notice progress and improvements in fitness. Using the burpee as an example, perform as many repetitions as possible within 30 seconds or a set of 10 to 15 repetitions. Ultimately, it's up to the coach and the athlete to determine which method works best. In either case, it's recommended that the athlete complete two to four sets of 10 to 15 repetitions with 1 to 2 minutes of rest between sets.

Burpee

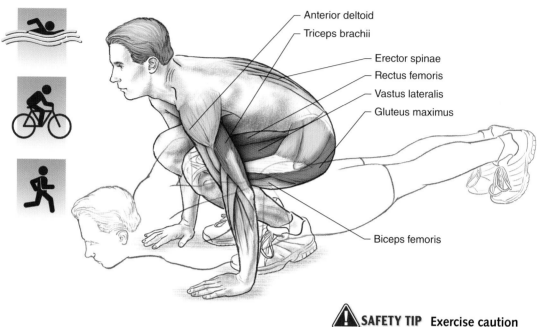

Anterior deltoid
Triceps brachii
Erector spinae
Rectus femoris
Vastus lateralis
Gluteus maximus
Biceps femoris

⚠ **SAFETY TIP** Exercise caution when performing the ballistic jumping motion. Knees should be slightly bent at the point of impact.

Execution

1. Start in a standing position with your feet shoulder-width apart. Place your hands on the ground.
2. Kick your legs out and assume a push-up position with a flat back. Lower yourself and perform a push-up while keeping your body straight. Forcibly push back up.
3. Draw your feet underneath your body and then explosively jump into the air as you extend your arms straight over your head.
4. Land on the ground with knees slightly bent. Perform the movement again for the required number of repetitions.

Muscles Involved

Primary: Quadriceps (rectus femoris, vastus lateralis, vastus intermedius, vastus medialis), gluteus maximus, pectoralis major, triceps brachii

Secondary: Hamstrings (biceps femoris, semitendinosus, semimembranosus), erector spinae, anterior deltoid

Triathlon Focus

The burpee is a great all-around exercise that will develop both cardiorespiratory and muscular strength and endurance as well as overall athleticism. Swimmers will benefit from increased upper-body strength as well as the ability to push more forcibly off the wall in training. Cyclists and runners will benefit from enhanced leg strength and power resulting from the jumps, as well as increasing overall dexterity and quickness.

As athletes quickly discover, a set of 10 to 15 repetitions will elicit a high heart rate and significant fitness gains when done with some consistency in a structured dryland training program.

Box Jump

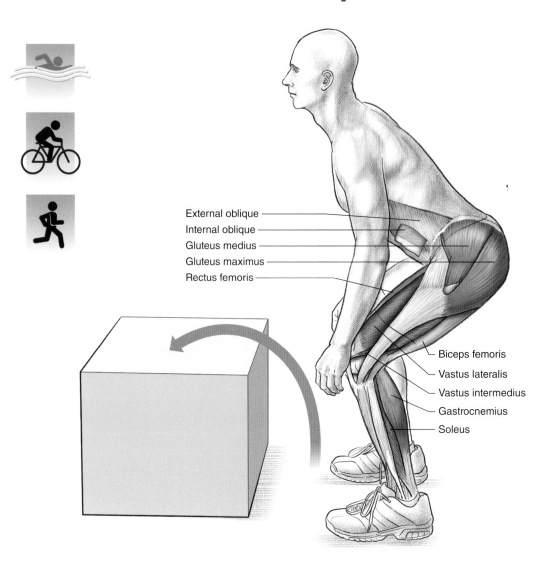

External oblique
Internal oblique
Gluteus medius
Gluteus maximus
Rectus femoris

Biceps femoris
Vastus lateralis
Vastus intermedius
Gastrocnemius
Soleus

Execution

1. Place a plyometric box, approximately knee height, firmly on the ground. Stand 6 to 8 inches (15 to 20 cm) from the box.
2. Launch yourself with a powerful jump onto the box. Land with your legs slightly bent.
3. Stand up straight on top of the box to finish the movement.
4. Step down to the starting position. Repeat for the required number of repetitions.

Muscles Involved

Primary: Quadriceps (rectus femoris, vastus medialis, vastus intermedius, vastus lateralis), gluteus maximus, gluteus medius, gastrocnemius, soleus

Secondary: Hamstrings (biceps femoris, semitendinosus, semimembranosus), external oblique, internal oblique, transversus abdominis, erector spinae

Triathlon Focus

Box jumps develop explosive power beneficial to cyclists and runners. Jumping up on the box provides a targeted challenge because the box height can be increased as jumping fitness and power improve over time.

Cyclists will benefit from this exercise by realizing more explosive power on climbs and in sprinting situations. Runners will develop the ability to drive with more power and speed up steep inclines.

Cheating in this exercise involves tucking the legs excessively to get to the box. If you find it necessary to tuck your legs, consider reducing the height of the box.

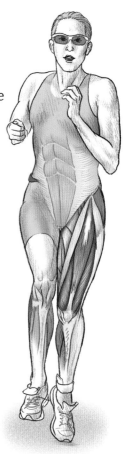

Woodchopper

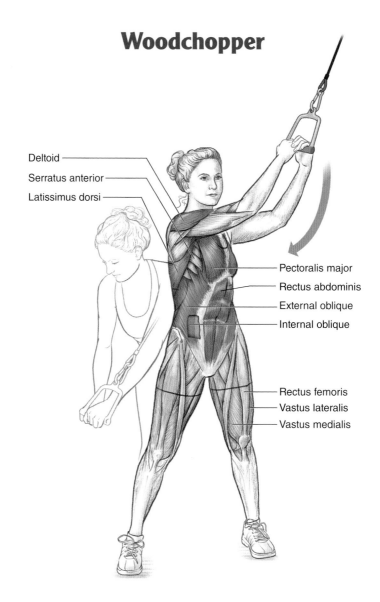

Deltoid
Serratus anterior
Latissimus dorsi

Pectoralis major
Rectus abdominis
External oblique
Internal oblique

Rectus femoris
Vastus lateralis
Vastus medialis

Execution

1. Stand sideways to a high-pulley machine, with your feet slightly wider than shoulder-width apart.
2. Grasp the handle with both hands.
3. Initiate the movement with the arm, shoulder, and chest muscles, pulling the handle diagonally down across your body.
4. Engage the core muscles while simultaneously bending your knees as you pull the handle toward the ground.
5. Slowly control the return to the starting position. Repeat for the required number of repetitions.

Muscles Involved

Primary: Rectus abdominis, internal oblique, external oblique, deltoid, latissimus dorsi, pectoralis major

Secondary: Quadriceps (rectus femoris, vastus lateralis, vastus medialis, vastus intermedius), gluteus medius, gluteus maximus, gluteus minimus, teres major, serratus anterior

Triathlon Focus

Multisport athletes require a strong core and coordination between upper-body and lower-body muscle groups. The woodchopper provides a dynamic full range of motion that engages several critical muscle groups while also promoting overall body coordination. Done properly and as part of a high-intensity workout, the exercise will also boost heart rate during its execution.

Specific to the needs of the competitive triathlete, this exercise also promotes greater core stability and endurance, especially useful for long-distance racing.

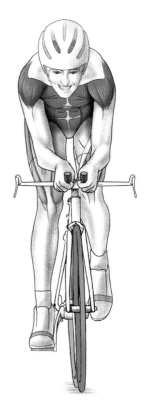

Reverse Woodchopper

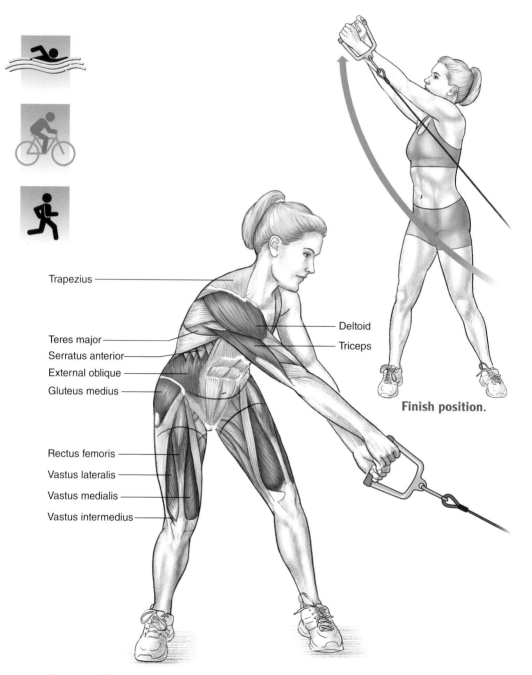

Trapezius

Deltoid

Triceps

Teres major

Serratus anterior

External oblique

Gluteus medius

Rectus femoris

Vastus lateralis

Vastus medialis

Vastus intermedius

Finish position.

Execution

1. Stand side-on to and about 3 feet (.9 m) away from a low-cable pulley machine, with your feet slightly wider than shoulder-width apart.

2. Slightly bend your knees into a half-squat position, and grab the pulley handle with both hands.

3. In a coordinated motion, raise the pulley handle diagonally across the body and over the opposite shoulder while standing straight.

4. Lower slowly to the starting position. Repeat for the required number of repetitions.

Muscles Involved

Primary: Quadriceps (rectus femoris, vastus medialis, vastus intermedius, vastus lateralis), gluteus maximus, gluteus medius, erector spinae, external oblique, internal oblique, deltoid, triceps brachii

Secondary: Hamstrings (biceps femoris, semitendinosus, semimembranosus), serratus anterior, teres major, trapezius, supraspinatus, rhomboid minor, rhomboid major

Triathlon Focus

This movement is particularly useful for swimmers as a dryland exercise but can also translate well for runners in building core, upper-arm, and leg strength. Runners are advised to bend slightly more at the knee to engage the quadriceps to a higher extent.

One important technique consideration is to engage the core muscle groups by focusing on the path the hand takes as it moves diagonally across the body. This will ensure maximum use of this important area.

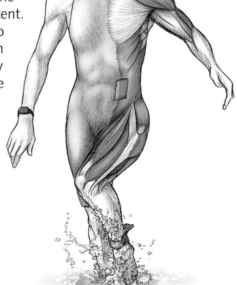

VARIATION

Diagonal Medicine Ball Lift

Using a medicine ball, initiate the movement much the same way as you would with a low-pulley cable machine. Emphasize power by explosively tossing the medicine ball over your shoulder to a partner with each repetition.

Double-Leg Power Jump

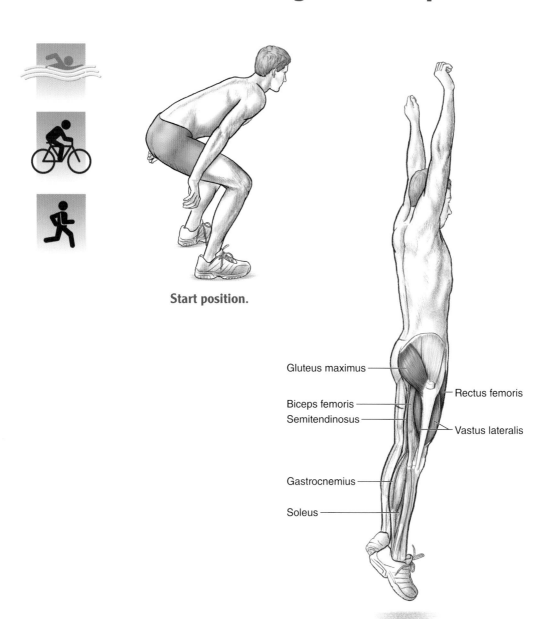

Start position.

Gluteus maximus

Rectus femoris

Biceps femoris

Semitendinosus

Vastus lateralis

Gastrocnemius

Soleus

Execution

1. With your feet slightly wider than shoulder-width apart, squat down with your knees bent at approximately 45-degree angles.
2. With explosive force, using the upward momentum of your arms and the power generated from your quadriceps, jump straight up and slightly forward to your maximal height.
3. Land and return to the original squat position. Repeat for the required number of repetitions.

Muscles Involved

Primary: Gluteus maximus, quadriceps (rectus femoris, vastus lateralis, vastus medialis, vastus intermedius)

Secondary: Erector spinae, hamstrings (biceps femoris, semitendinosus, semimembranosus), soleus, gastrocnemius, hip adductors

Triathlon Focus

The ability to produce explosive power is a key to success in all sporting activities, including endurance-focused cycling and running. The power jump is simplicity at its finest, producing huge gains in explosive leg power without the need for fancy or expensive exercise equipment.

Because this is a highly dynamic exercise, it's important to perform the power jump with very warm muscles. Pay special attention to the landing on each repetition, which should be soft and under control. Athletes of all levels will benefit from increased power as well as the cardiorespiratory gains this challenging exercise has to offer.

For the competitive triathlete, enhanced power through doing power jumps can improve short-burst speed for climbing steep hills on the bike and powering up the hills on the run.

Lunge With Biceps Curl

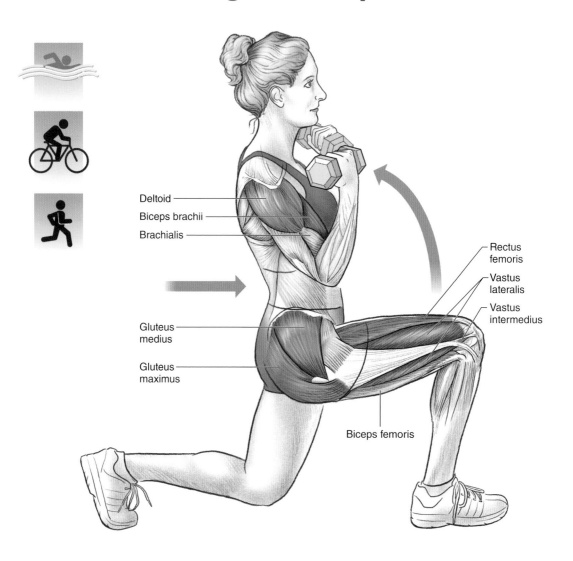

Deltoid

Biceps brachii

Brachialis

Rectus femoris

Vastus lateralis

Vastus intermedius

Gluteus medius

Gluteus maximus

Biceps femoris

Execution

1. Start by holding a dumbbell in each hand, with the arms extended down at the sides. Stand erect with the feet shoulder-width apart.

2. Step forward with one leg into a lunge position.

3. Once in lunge position and holding it steady, curl the weights up and lower them.

4. Stand up to the starting position, and repeat with the opposite leg. Do this for the required number of repetitions.

Muscles Involved

Primary: Quadriceps (rectus femoris, vastus lateralis, vastus medialis, vastus intermedius), gluteus medius, gluteus maximus, deltoid, biceps brachii

Secondary: Hamstrings (biceps femoris, semitendinosus, semimembranosus), brachialis, forearms

Triathlon Focus

Multijoint, full-body exercises such as the lunge with biceps curl serve the triathlete by maximizing training time effectiveness. The lunge is a key exercise for the endurance athlete in terms of developing strength and power in the lower body, while the biceps curl targets the muscles in the upper and lower arms and, to some extent, the shoulders.

Cyclists will benefit from the ability to pull forcibly against the handlebars when climbing or sprinting. Runners will have the enhanced ability to drive with the arms when running up a steep hill.

Squat Press

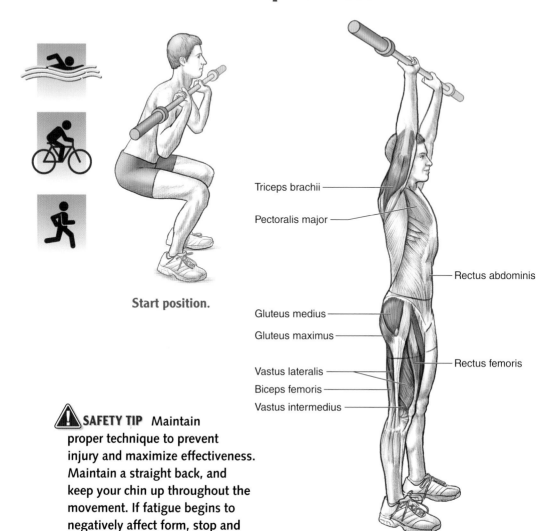

Start position.

Triceps brachii

Pectoralis major

Rectus abdominis

Gluteus medius

Gluteus maximus

Vastus lateralis

Biceps femoris

Vastus intermedius

Rectus femoris

⚠ **SAFETY TIP** Maintain proper technique to prevent injury and maximize effectiveness. Maintain a straight back, and keep your chin up throughout the movement. If fatigue begins to negatively affect form, stop and rest or move to another activity.

Execution

1. Stand erect with feet shoulder-width apart. Grasp a barbell across your upper chest, with your palms turned out.
2. Bend to a squatting position, with your upper quadriceps almost parallel to the ground.
3. Extend up into a standing position. From there, press the weight over your head, and then lower it in a controlled manner.
4. Lower back to the squat position. Repeat for the required number of repetitions

Muscles Involved

Primary: Quadriceps (rectus femoris, vastus lateralis, vastus medialis, vastus intermedius), gluteus maximus, gluteus minimus, gluteus medius, anterior deltoid, triceps brachii

Secondary: Hip adductors, hamstrings (biceps femoris, semitendinosus, semimembranosus), erector spinae, trapezius, rectus abdominis, upper pectoralis major

Triathlon Focus

This whole-body exercise combines the effectiveness of the squat with that of the shoulder press, making for a demanding and result-producing movement. Multisport athletes will benefit from enhanced leg and shoulder strength for improved swimming, cycling, and running performance at all levels. Furthermore, the combination of two major muscle group exercises increases time effectiveness and efficiency while also enhancing coordination.

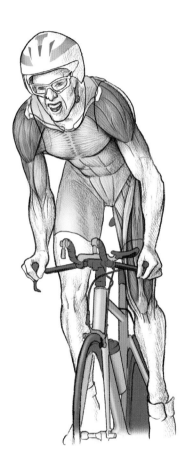

Floor Wiper

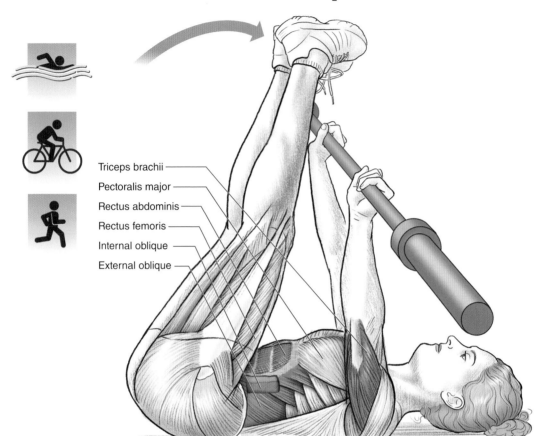

Triceps brachii
Pectoralis major
Rectus abdominis
Rectus femoris
Internal oblique
External oblique

Execution

1. Lie flat on your back on the floor.
2. Hold a barbell over your chest, with your arms fully extended.
3. Raise your legs, keeping them as straight as possible, although you may need to bend your knees slightly.
4. While keeping your upper body stable, lower your legs to one end of the bar, and then sweep them to the other end of the bar in a wiping motion.
5. Repeat for the required number of repetitions.

Muscles Involved

Primary: Rectus abdominis, external oblique, internal oblique, triceps brachii

Secondary: Pectineus, sartorius, iliopsoas, rectus femoris, pectoralis major

Triathlon Focus

The floor wiper is a challenging exercise that does a great job of engaging the core muscle groups. This benefits the triathlete by increasing the ability to rotate with force and authority. This is especially useful in freestyle swimming in which coordinated body rotation is so important as well as when climbing or sprinting hard on the bike. This exercise will test even the most conditioned athlete and take his core fitness to the next level.

Weighted Swing

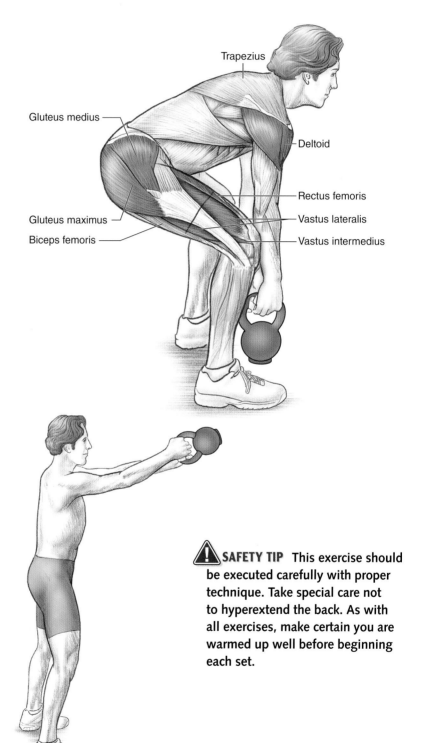

Trapezius

Gluteus medius

Deltoid

Rectus femoris

Vastus lateralis

Gluteus maximus

Vastus intermedius

Biceps femoris

SAFETY TIP This exercise should be executed carefully with proper technique. Take special care not to hyperextend the back. As with all exercises, make certain you are warmed up well before beginning each set.

Finish position.

Execution

1. Set a kettlebell, medicine ball, dumbbell, or plate of an appropriate weight between your legs. Stand with feet slightly wider than shoulder-width apart.
2. Bend over with a straight back, and grasp the weight with both hands.
3. Initiate the movement by forcefully standing to an erect position, engaging your legs and core, while lifting the weight from the floor.
4. Using the momentum created by the explosive effort and keeping the arms straight, bring the kettlebell up to eye level.
5. Return the kettlebell to its starting position, again with your knees bent. Repeat for the required number of repetitions.

Muscles Involved

Primary: Quadriceps (rectus femoris, vastus lateralis, vastus medialis, vastus intermedius), gluteus maximus, gluteus minimus, gluteus medius, deltoid, erector spinae, rectus abdominis

Secondary: Hip adductors, trapezius, hamstrings (biceps femoris, semitendinosus, semimembranosus), forearms, pectoralis major

Triathlon Focus

Another whole-body exercise that engages a large number of muscle groups, the weighted swing encourages the development of explosive power and overall coordination. This is especially helpful to the triathlete who must begin a race aggressively when the mass open-water swim starts, attack a hill with vigor, or sprint to the finish line. For example, a beach start for the swim requires high stepping and dolphin diving into the surf, which requires the strength and coordination developed from the performance of this exercise.

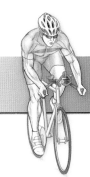

INJURY PREVENTION

No discussion of training programs would be complete without examining both their pros and cons. For all the good that we have proposed in the previous chapters, there are inherent risks with trying to get stronger and faster. The body is designed to respond to exercise stress by

- enhancing the cellular mechanism to sustain aerobic and anaerobic metabolism;
- improving the cardiorespiratory system to supply oxygen and nutrients to tissues;
- increasing muscular cell size and strength; and
- strengthening the tissues of tendons, ligaments, and bones to support the athletic loads placed on them.

The problem is that an athlete can reach a point at which this enhancement is disrupted, which may cause injury. This event is initiated by tissue failure in the form of tearing at both a microscopic and sometimes visible, or macroscopic, level that causes a cascade of actions including localized bleeding from damaged vessels and recruitment of cells that promote healing. This process can take anywhere from 4 to 6 weeks to complete. Some tissues may take longer depending on a variety of factors including the magnitude of the initial injury and the promptness of treatment. Healing may take longer if any injury becomes chronic.

Types of Injury

Trauma, which is defined as a significant force applied to normal tissue, such as falling from a bike, can cause injury. This is somewhat intuitive, but the result varies in severity. A simple bruise, or contusion, from soft-tissue injury can cause localized bleeding and swelling. More significant force can lead to a broken, or fractured, bone. This is often accompanied by a visible deformity, as with a clavicle fracture.

Triathlon participation is somewhat unique in that we train in more than one sport. If we stay upright on the bike, traumatic injuries are rare. However, because of the nature of endurance sports and the repetitive stresses we place on our tissues, overuse injuries are more common for triathletes than for those who participate in many single sports.

An overuse injury can be defined as failure of a tissue—including muscles, tendons, ligaments, and even bone—at less than maximal force. Think of a coat hanger, a relatively strong piece of metal. If you were to take it and start bending it with only a small amount of force, eventually it would break. Collagen, which makes up 70 percent of the dry weight of the body, is vulnerable to this type of tissue failure. If you pull hard enough on a rope, eventually some of its fibers will tear. If you pull long enough and hard enough, the entire rope may tear. All our tissues have cellular mechanisms that are constantly defending against and attempting to repair these injuries. Exercising can challenge the equilibrium between the process of strengthening and getting faster and the process of repairing the structural breakdown of tissues. Sometimes this can be like walking on thin ice. As you push the envelope of training, such as by trying to catch up on a workout, run more during a week than you are used to, or swim with paddles when your arms are tired, the risk of injury increases. Many other instances can lead us down the wrong path. We have all been there and done that. The advantage of training for a triathlon as opposed to a single sport is that triathlon workouts emphasize a different part of the body on any given day and allow us to rest and heal an area that may be at risk for injury.

Prevention and Recognition of Injuries

Rest, which by nature triathletes are inherently bad at, is an integral part of the healing process. This is when the body heals itself and gets stronger, whether you are taking a day or a few weeks off from working out or reducing the intensity or volume of your workouts. Prevention techniques that assist with healing, including stretching and specific strengthening, are often overlooked but are an essential part of triathlon training.

Injuries are not an act of nature. They indicate that the athlete has reached a breakdown point at which the body can no longer respond in a positive fashion and heal the injury. The body is pushed past its reparative capabilities and begins to develop signs and symptoms of injury. One of the hallmark symptoms of injury is pain. We all have experienced discomfort when working out, but when is it bad to push through the discomfort? Pain can be defined as an unpleasant sensation that is often associated with damage to the body. What about the sayings "Pain is just weakness leaving the body" and "No pain, no gain"? These proverbs are fun to say but if practiced can lead you down the path of chronic injury.

Any discomfort may be an early warning sign of injury. Discomfort that begins with an activity but goes away as you warm up may be an acceptable symptom you are able to train through with appropriate modifications. However, discomfort that continues through the activity should be a clear warning sign that something is not right, and activity should be discontinued. Discomfort that persists after the activity, does not respond to the basic treatment of RICE (rest, ice, compression, elevation), and affects other functions including activities of daily living should be treated and, if necessary, evaluated by a sports medicine specialist.

The ability to recognize when something is wrong is the first step to treating the injury. Maturity and experience help this process. A qualified coach or trainer can help you develop appropriate workouts; a well-designed training plan can minimize the chance for injury. Keeping a training log is also important so you can look back and see if a specific workout or series of workouts was the precipitating agent of injury.

Overuse injuries are particularly difficult to recognize. Often there is no one single event that causes the injury. Over a period of time the discomfort gradually becomes debilitating. Many of these injuries lack some of the signs of acute injury including bleeding, swelling, and tenderness. They just cause discomfort and pain when you want to swim, bike, and run.

Treatment

Treatment of injuries relies on a simple principle: Treat the cause as well as the effect. Mistakes in training plans can be corrected. Equipment or technique issues such as poor swim stroke mechanics, improper bike fit, and worn-out sneakers should be considered. Nutrition issues also play a role in injury prevention and treatment. Diets deficient in protein and adequate carbohydrate fail to address the nutrition demands placed on the body during strenuous exercise. This is demonstrated in the female athlete triad, in which eating disorders, lower than optimal body weight, and abnormal menstruation due to loss of proper hormonal control lead to the development of stress-related injuries to bone, including stress fractures.

The RICE approach, which stands for rest, ice, compression, and elevation, applies to the basic treatment of any injury. If rest is a bad word to you, try *relative rest*, during which you perform alternative activities (cross-train) that cause no discomfort.

Use ice on an acute injury of any type for the first 36 to 48 hours. After that it can be very useful for pain control. Apply ice to the affected area for 10 to 15 minutes every 2 to 3 hours. Protect the skin with a piece of light fabric to prevent complications associated with ice, including skin burn. You may apply heat after the first 48 hours when stiffness may be present. Application principles are similar. No scientific literature supports alternating the two treatments; therefore it is not recommended.

Compression is helpful to control swelling. In an acute situation, compression helps control bleeding and thus swelling. Wrapping the affected area comfortably with an elastic bandage can be effective for as long as tolerated.

Elevation is helpful for extremity injuries as it also helps control swelling. Be sure to place the affected area above the level of the heart to allow the swelling to drain.

Stretches for Injury Prevention and Treatment

Injury prevention requires a well-designed training plan with periods of rest and nutrition guidance for preworkout, in-workout, and postworkout consumption. Another important piece of the puzzle is a stretching program. Exercise places a great deal of stress on the tissues, which can lead to stiffness. This may lead to loss of motion about the joint and cause a change in biomechanics, which can lead to injury.

Stretching needs to be part of any successful exercise program. Stretches can be performed both before and after workouts. A short warm-up of 5 to 10 minutes of light aerobic exercise may prevent injury when stretching before a workout. Muscles are probably more receptive to stretching after a workout. Amazingly, there is a lack of scientific evidence as to the duration of stretching or to its exact benefits; however, experts and athletes alike believe that if it feels good, it is probably doing some good.

Dynamic Stretching

Dynamic stretching is a popular form of stretching among athletes and is recommended before engaging in training activities. Contrary to static stretching (stretch and hold), which is best performed after activities or as part of a cool-down, dynamic stretching includes a gentle and progressive active movement pattern throughout a comfortable range of motion, not exceeding that of a static stretch. Going beyond that range would be considered a ballistic stretch, which is not recommended. Dynamic stretching offers numerous benefits including increasing range of motion, increasing temperature, improving blood and oxygen flow to areas specific to the training activity, enhancing the nervous system and motor ability in preparation for training, and preventing training-related injuries.

Performing a dynamic stretch is simple but requires caution. Begin with a short range of motion. As you warm up, increase the range of motion toward your maximum level. The walking lunge and carioca are two examples of dynamic stretches popular among triathletes and runners. For the walking lunge, stand with feet shoulder-width apart, and step forward with the leading foot to assume a lunge position. Supporting your body weight on your leading foot, stand erect again and step forward with the opposite foot. Repeat this series of walking lunges for 10 steps with each leg and repeat. The carioca is a good dynamic stretch that targets the hips and other areas of lateral movement. Stand with feet shoulder-width apart and knees slightly bent. Cross the left foot over and in front of the right foot. Repeat with the right foot crossing the left foot in a lateral movement, gently twisting at the hips. Travel for 30 to 50 feet (10 to 15 m) in one direction and then the other.

Incorporating dynamic stretching as part of your training preparation will pay off in reducing risk of injury and enhancing your training performance.

Basic Stretching

The basic stretches that follow are specific to the muscles used in triathlon training. They should be considered essential in the prevention of overuse injuries that can be sustained with triathlon participation. Stretching technique includes gentle motion until an easy stretch is felt. Hold the position for 15 to 30 seconds, and repeat two or three times. Bouncing, what was once referred to as ballistic stretching, can be detrimental and is not recommended.

Spend some time doing these gentle stretches. They feel good, help improve range of motion, and help you recover from injury.

Side Neck Stretch

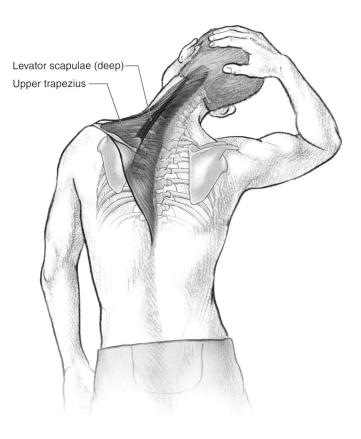

Levator scapulae (deep)
Upper trapezius

Execution

1. Sit or stand straight. Place one hand over your head toward the opposite ear.
2. Gently pull your hand to the side. Keep looking forward, and feel a stretch in the lateral neck region on the opposite side of the hand on your head.
3. Allow that shoulder to gently drop to help accentuate the stretch.
4. Hold this position for 15 to 30 seconds. Repeat three times on each side.

Muscles Involved

Primary: Upper trapezius

Secondary: Scalenes, levator scapulae

Triathlon Focus

A triathlete's head position changes constantly depending on the discipline. Adequate neck flexibility is imperative. Open-water freestyle swimming requires the ability to sight buoys. Swimmers must look up frequently as well as switch breathing pattern from side to side. Riding in an aerodynamic tuck while cycling can create neck fatigue and strain along the back of the neck. Runners must have the neck strength and flexibility to maintain a neutral head and back position for maximum proficiency.

Arm on Wall Forward Stretch

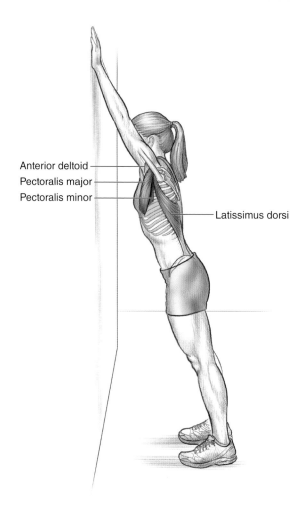

Anterior deltoid
Pectoralis major
Pectoralis minor

Latissimus dorsi

Execution

1. Stand 1 to 2 feet (.3 to .6 m) away from and facing a wall.
2. Walk the fingers of one arm up the wall until you feel a stretch along the chest and upper arm.
3. You may lean forward to increase the stretch.
4. Hold this position for 15 to 30 seconds. Repeat three times on each side.

Muscles Involved

Primary: Pectoralis major, pectoralis minor, latissimus dorsi

Secondary: Anterior deltoid

Triathlon Focus

Open-water distance freestyle swimming requires the triathlete to take long, steady strokes, maximizing distance per stroke and efficiency. Flexibility training for the chest and upper back assist the triathlete's ability to reach, helping him achieve optimal body rotation and glide.

Triceps Stretch

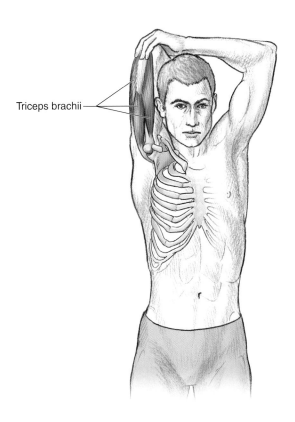

Triceps brachii

Execution

1. From a standing position, place one hand on the upper back of the opposite shoulder.
2. With the elbow bent toward the ceiling, use your other hand to pull the elbow toward your head.
3. Hold this position for 15 to 30 seconds. Repeat three times on each side.

Muscles Involved

Primary: Triceps brachii

Triathlon Focus

Open-water freestyle swimming engages the triceps in a key propulsive phase of the swim stroke. Cyclists require extensive use of the triceps when climbing aggressively out of the saddle.

181

Chest Stretch

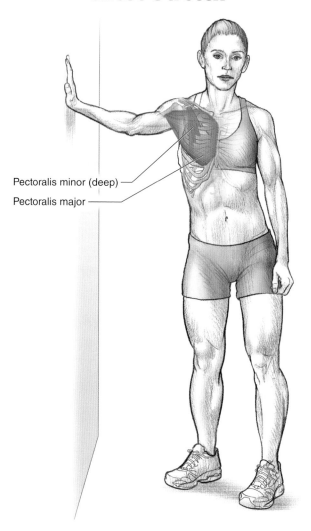

Pectoralis minor (deep)

Pectoralis major

Execution

1. Stand in a doorway or next to a wall.
2. Place the hand of the arm to be stretched on the wall or doorjamb.
3. Rotate your body away from the hand, and feel the stretch in the front of the shoulder.
4. Hold this position for 15 to 30 seconds. Repeat three times on each side.

Muscles Involved

Primary: Pectoralis major

Secondary: Pectoralis minor

Triathlon Focus

Stretching the chest benefits each sport discipline for the triathlete. Swimmers realize greater arm extension and have the ability to get long and streamlined during each stroke. Cyclists enjoy an enhanced ability to ride out of the saddle when grasping the drops or the base-bar handles. Runners can drive with their arms when charging up steep inclines.

Standing Hamstring Stretch

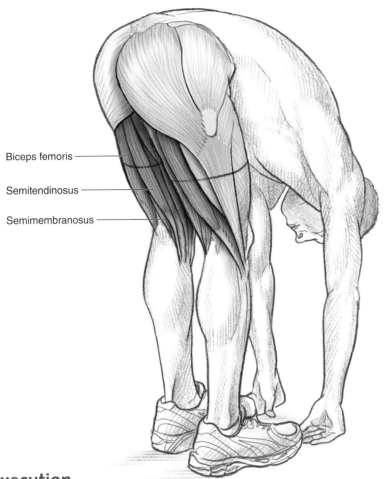

Biceps femoris

Semitendinosus

Semimembranosus

Execution

1. Stand with your feet together, knees slightly bent.
2. Slowly roll forward from your neck to your lower back. Use your hands to help support your upper body.
3. Continue moving down until you begin to feel a gentle stretch in the backs of your thighs and in your lower back. Release your hands to the floor.
4. Hold this position for 15 to 30 seconds. Repeat three times.

Muscles Involved

Primary: Hamstrings (biceps femoris, semitendinosus, semimembranosus)

Secondary: Lower-back muscles, paraspinals

Triathlon Focus

For the triathlete, hamstring flexibility is imperative. Cyclists require flexible hamstrings to achieve a proper aerodynamic position. Runners will find that more flexible hamstrings provide for a greater range of motion, especially during a surge or sprint to the finish line.

183

Adductor Stretch

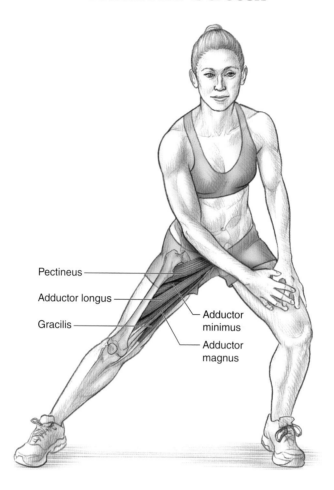

Pectineus

Adductor longus

Gracilis

Adductor minimus

Adductor magnus

Execution

1. Stand with feet slightly wider than shoulder-width apart.
2. Keeping the right leg straight, bend your left knee. Use your hands for support. Lean to the left.
3. You should feel a stretch in the right inner thigh.
4. Hold this position for 15 to 30 seconds. Repeat three times on each side.

Muscles Involved

Primary: Adductor longus, adductor magnus, adductor minimus, gracilis, pectineus

Triathlon Focus

Greater flexibility in the adductors helps improve cycling and running form while reducing chance of injury. Off-road triathlon events that include trail running will be sure to place additional stress on this area.

Hip Rotation Stretch

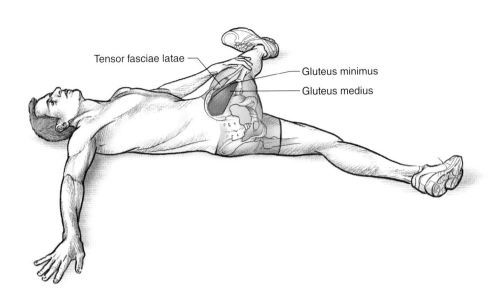

Tensor fasciae latae

Gluteus minimus

Gluteus medius

Execution

1. Lie on the floor on your back, legs straight.
2. Bring the right leg over the left leg, keeping the legs straight or only slightly bent.
3. Use your left hand to pull the right knee across your body.
4. You should feel the stretch in the buttocks and posterior hip.
5. Hold this position for 15 to 30 seconds. Repeat three times on each side.

Muscles Involved

Primary: Gluteus medius, gluteus minimus

Secondary: Tensor fasciae latae

Triathlon Focus

For the triathlete, enhanced hip-region flexibility can help prevent a number of lower-body issues related to the twisting and turning a triathlete does in the execution of open-water swimming, transitions, and aggressive running.

Therapeutic Stretching

This series of therapeutic stretching exercises is intended to help manage symptoms associated with a variety of overuse injuries that occur with triathlon participation. The stretching technique includes gentle motion until an easy stretch is felt. Hold the position for 15 to 30 seconds, and repeat two or three times. Bouncing, once referred to as ballistic stretching, can be detrimental and is not recommended. If you experience pain or discomfort while doing the stretch, ease back and apply less pressure. A sense of pulling is appropriate, but that must be distinguished from pain. If pain persists and a stretch cannot be performed without discomfort, professional assistance may be necessary.

Cross-Body Arm Stretch

Execution

1. From a standing or seated position, take the affected arm and cross it horizontally over the chest.
2. Place the other hand on the elbow, and gently assist the stretch across the body.
3. You will feel a pulling sensation on the back of the shoulder.
4. Hold this position for 15 to 30 seconds. Repeat three times on each side.

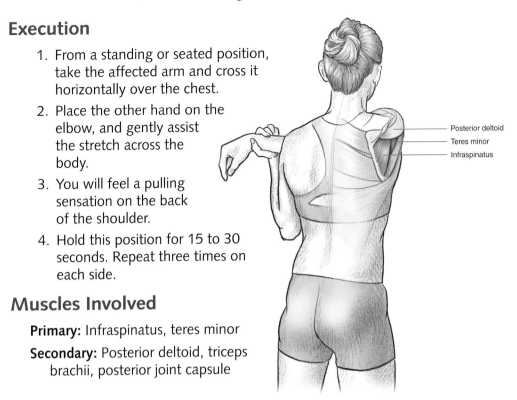

Posterior deltoid
Teres minor
Infraspinatus

Muscles Involved

Primary: Infraspinatus, teres minor

Secondary: Posterior deltoid, triceps brachii, posterior joint capsule

Triathlon Focus

The rotator cuff, discussed in chapter 5, helps control shoulder motion. Performing overhead activities including swimming can cause an overuse or microscopic injury to the tendons of the rotator cuff and the tissues that lie adjacent to it, including the bursa. Using poor swim technique such as crossing the arm over the midline on hand entry or participating in a harder than normal swim workout can cause such an injury. The bursa can become irritated and inflamed if the rotator cuff is not functioning in a coordinated fashion. This stretch can help reduce stiffness of the shoulder joint and reduce pain. Stretching the capsule and rotator cuff tendons coupled with rotator cuff strengthening exercises, such as the internal and external rotation exercises in chapter 5, can also help reduce pain and increase function. Shoulder muscle imbalances and poor posture can predispose or exacerbate the condition. Exercises to improve posture and maintain shoulder biomechanics, including those that strengthen the posterior muscles of the shoulder and back, can help prevent impingement from occurring. See chapter 5 for the single-arm dumbbell row as well as chapter 8 for the lat pull-down.

Quadriceps Stretch

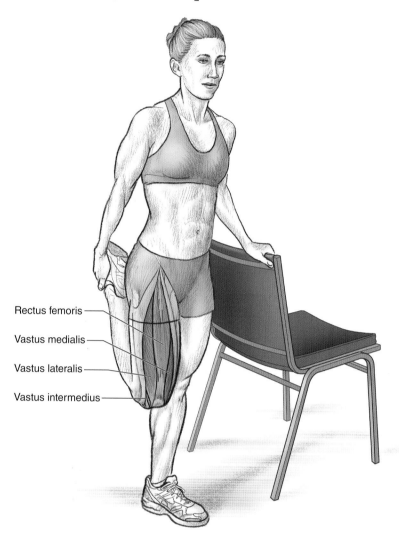

Rectus femoris
Vastus medialis
Vastus lateralis
Vastus intermedius

Execution

1. Using a wall or steady piece of furniture for support, bend your right leg and try to grab your ankle. If this is difficult, loop a towel around your ankle. Keep your knees together. Do not arch your back.

2. Gently bring your heel toward your buttocks. Push your hips forward to accentuate the stretch. You should feel a stretch in the front of your thigh (quadriceps) muscle.

3. Hold the stretch for 15 to 30 seconds. Repeat with the other leg.

Muscles Involved

Primary: Quadriceps (rectus femoris, vastus medialis, vastus lateralis, vastus intermedius)

Triathlon Focus

Running and biking place large forces on the joints of the lower extremities, especially the knee. The patella, kneecap, and peripatellar tissues are exposed to approximately three to five times body weight with such activities. Forces to your tissues that exceed the body's ability to tolerate them can cause injury and pain. Often there is no single identifiable cause, but repetitive microscopic trauma can result in an overuse injury. Changes in training including increased volume, intensity, or duration can be a contributing factor. Worn-out or ill-fitting running shoes or a drastic change in footwear are also factors that can lead to increased stresses on the knee. Anterior knee pain, which is often characterized as diffuse and under the kneecap, is just one of the symptoms caused by this condition, often referred to as runner's knee. Activities of daily living such as stair walking and sitting with the legs bent (e.g., sitting for a long time at the movies) can cause similar symptoms.

The quadriceps muscles and the tissues around the knee often become tight and contracted. Stretching the quadriceps will restore flexibility and improve knee symptoms. Improved core stability and strong lower extremities can help address muscular imbalances that lead to altered biomechanics and result in symptoms of runner's knee. Strength exercises found in chapter 8, including the floor bridge, and chapter 9, wall stability-ball squat, are essential for the process of rehabilitation.

Single Leg to Chest Stretch

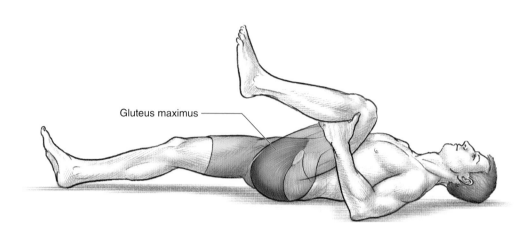

Gluteus maximus

Execution

1. Lie on your back.
2. With your hands behind your left leg, gently pull your left knee to your chest until you feel a comfortable stretch in the low back and buttocks.
3. Hold this position for 15 to 30 seconds. Repeat three times on each leg.

Muscles Involved

Primary: Gluteus maximus

Secondary: Erector spinae

Triathlon Focus

Injuries to the muscles of the lower back are common in both athletic and nonathletic people. Improper bike fit including an overly aggressive aerodynamic position and even basic running can strain the muscles, tendons, and ligaments of the lower back. Mechanical low-back pain is different from radicular or neurological pain, which is caused by nerve irritation, most commonly from a herniated disc. Localized back pain and stiffness are two of the most common symptoms of a mechanical muscle strain. Leg pain, numbness, weakness, or tingling of the leg can be signs of a herniated disc. The muscles of the lower back and legs, including the erector spinae, multifidus, and hamstrings, can become tight. Gentle stretching of the lower back can help increase flexibility and ease symptoms.

Piriformis Stretch

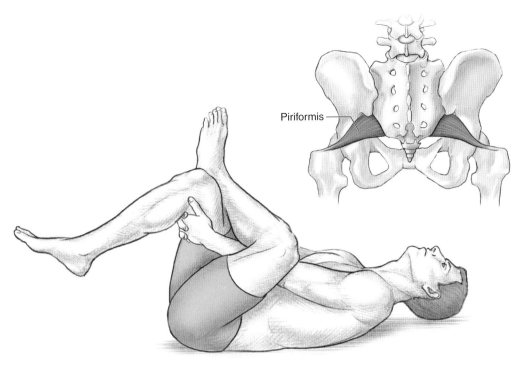

Piriformis

Execution

1. Lie on your back, and cross your left ankle over your right thigh.
2. Using your hands, pull your right thigh up while bending the right hip. You should feel a stretch in the left buttocks.
3. If able, use the left hand or elbow to push your left knee out. This may accentuate the stretch.
4. Hold the stretch for 15 to 30 seconds and switch legs.

Muscles Involved

Primary: Piriformis

Triathlon Focus

The piriformis muscle is exposed to significant stress during running. Repetitive forward motion can cause muscle imbalances from overdeveloped hip flexors and relatively weak hip abductors and adductors. This can cause the piriformis to contract and shorten. The sciatica nerve or large groups of nerve roots that run down the leg can be compressed as they pass under the piriformis muscle and tendon in the deep buttock. This can cause pain, tingling, and numbness down the leg. Although buttock pain is caused by many conditions, including hamstring strains and sciatica, piriformis syndrome can be an elusive diagnosis. Tightness of this muscle also occurs after sitting in the saddle for a long time. Prevention and treatment of injury with appropriate stretching is time well spent. Strength training of the abductors and adductors can also be therapeutic. See chapter 9 for machine abduction and adduction.

Iliotibial Band Stretch

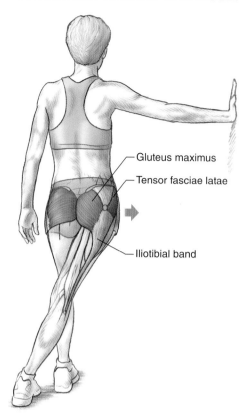

Gluteus maximus

Tensor fasciae latae

Iliotibial band

Execution

1. Stand next to a wall. Place the right hand on the wall for support.
2. Cross the right leg behind the left leg.
3. Without bending forward, lean both hips into the wall.
4. Hold this position for 15 seconds. Repeat three times on each side.

Muscles Involved

Primary: Iliotibial band, tensor fasciae latae, gluteus maximus

Triathlon Focus

In iliotibial band friction syndrome, pain and stiffness occurring on the outer aspect of the knee during running can be the hallmark of trouble to come. The iliotibial, or IT, band originates about the hip and tensor fasciae latae, extends down the thigh, and attaches to the knee. The IT band makes two potential contact points at the hip (the greater trochanter) and knee (the lateral epicondyle). Between each contact point, a bursal sac helps provide smooth motion over the bony prominences. Injury, irritation, or tissue tightness can increase friction that can cause inflammation and subsequent pain about the knee; disabling discomfort can occur if symptoms are left untreated. Stretching the iliotibial band is an essential part of any preventative or treatment plan. Additional strength training of the hip abductors and core is thought to decrease risk of developing IT band friction syndrome.

Tibialis Anterior Stretch

Execution

1. Kneel on both legs on a soft surface for comfort.

2. Point your toes so that the tops of the feet and legs rest on the ground.

3. Use your hands to push the legs closer to the ground, or if comfortable, you can sit on your heels.

4. Hold this position for 15 to 30 seconds. Repeat three times.

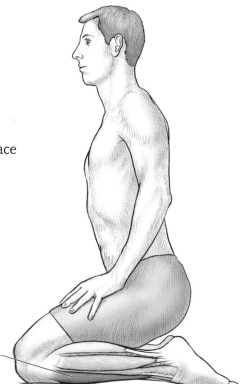

Adductor magnus

Muscles Involved

Primary: Tibialis anterior

Triathlon Focus

Running requires complex motion about the ankle and foot. The tibialis anterior provides ankle dorsiflexion and allows the runner to clear the foot as he swings the leg forward. As the runner puts the foot down and makes contact with the ground, the foot is relatively flexible so as to absorb shock and accommodate changes in the surface.

The posterior tibialis muscle and tendon along with the calf muscles help absorb the impact and prepare for the push-off phase of gait. As the ankle and foot roll forward to push off, the posterior tibialis contracts, causing its tendon to lock the ankle and foot and create a strong platform that transmits force and allows for push-off. The posterior tibialis inserts along the shaft of the inner aspect of the tibia. Its tendon runs down the lower leg and wraps around the inner ankle to insert on the foot. Because this muscle is essential for running, repetitive stress at the site of muscle insertion, the periosteum, can cause tearing and inflammation.

Tightness of the anterior tibialis, which commonly occurs with running, can cause abnormal stress on the posterior tibialis. This can cause diffuse discomfort along the inner tibia at the beginning of a run. Stretching of both the calf muscles and the tibialis anterior can help alleviate this problem.

Foot Stretch

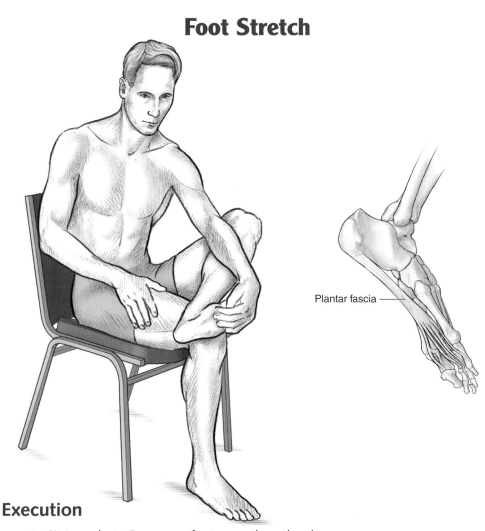

Plantar fascia

Execution

1. Sit in a chair. Cross one foot over the other knee.
2. Using the hand, gently pull the toes up. The ankle may also move.
3. Hold for 15 to 30 seconds. Repeat three times for each foot.

Muscles Involved

Primary: Plantar fascia

Secondary: Intrinsic muscles of the foot

Triathlon Focus

For an athlete, heel pain can be the bane of her existence. Walking, sitting, even getting out of bed can be problematic. Microscopic injury to the insertion of a layer of tissue at the bottom of the foot into the heel, the plantar fascia, can be disabling. Repetitive impact loading from running, wearing worn-out shoes, or just having bad luck can cause plantar fasciitis to rear its ugly head. Improperly referred to as heel spurs, this condition takes a great deal of tender loving care to treat. This stretching exercise is just one of many techniques to reduce symptoms and allow for proper healing. Other treatments include ice, heel inserts, night splints, physical therapy, orthotics, new shoes, and medication.

Calf Stretch

Execution

1. Face a wall or steady piece of furniture. Use the hands for support.

2. Place the right leg close to the wall and the left leg comfortably 1 to 2 feet (.3 to .6 m) behind.

3. Keep the back leg straight and the heel firmly on the ground. Hips should be straight and facing the wall.

4. Gently lean the hips toward the wall until you feel a gentle pull in the calf of the back leg.

5. Hold this position for 15 to 30 seconds. Repeat three times for each leg.

Gastrocnemius

Soleus

Muscles Involved

Primary: Gastrocnemius

Secondary: Soleus, flexor hallucis longus, flexor digitorum longus

Triathlon Focus

Injury to the Achilles tendon, the largest tendon in the body, can cause symptoms of stiffness around the ankle as well as pain with motion. For the unfortunate athlete who sustains a complete rupture of the Achilles tendon, there are often no warning signs. Inflammation around the area causing swelling and possibly the development of a hard bump on the tendon can cause significant disturbance in athletic activities. The calf muscles—the gastrocnemius and soleus—together form the Achilles tendon. Injury to this region should be addressed with appropriate stretches such as this one. Strength training as described in chapter 9, such as the single-leg heel raise with dumbbells, can help treat and prevent muscle and tendon injury.

EXERCISE FINDER

Whole-Body Training

Injury Prevention

Basic Stretching

Therapeutic Stretching

ABOUT THE AUTHORS

Mark Klion, MD, is a board-certified orthopedic surgeon and sports medicine specialist. After receiving a bachelor's degree from St. Lawrence University in upstate New York, he earned his medical degree from the Mount Sinai School of Medicine in New York City. He completed his residency in orthopedic surgery at Mount Sinai Hospital. He then completed a sports medicine fellowship at the University of Chicago. During his fellowship, he specialized in arthroscopic surgery and reconstructive knee and shoulder surgery. He is a clinical instructor at the Mount Sinai School of Medicine and a member of their shoulder and sports medicine service. He serves as an educator for the medical school and the department of orthopedic surgery. He is also the director of orthopedics at St. Barnabas Hospital in New York. He performs the newest techniques for cartilage repair, regeneration, and meniscal transplantation. Dr. Klion has extensive experience with arthroscopic rotator cuff repairs and shoulder stabilization procedures.

Dr. Klion is also an avid triathlete and marathon runner. He has completed 10 Ironman triathlons, including Hawaii Ironmans in 2000 and 2001. He has completed 15 marathons and several ultradistance races. He created the DVD series *BodyworksMD*, a physician-guided physical therapy rehabilitation program. He serves as the medical codirector for the New York City Triathlon and Toughman Half Ironman and is the orthopedic consultant for the Triathlon Academy and Foundation bicycle team.

Troy Jacobson has been a leader in the field of triathlon coaching since 1992. He is the owner of Lifesports, Inc., an endurance multisport coaching company, and is recognized as a pioneer in developing and marketing online coaching services. He is the innovator and driving force behind the popular endurance sport training DVD *Spinervals Cycling* and founded the National Triathlon Academy in 2000. He created Train Right software, an intuitive coaching program chosen as the official software of Tri-Fed USA in the mid 1990s.

When Tri-Fed became USA Triathlon, Jacobson became a member of the inaugural USA Triathlon coaching committee. A personal coach to athletes of all abilities from age groupers to a former U.S. Olympian, Jacobson served as the official coach of Ironman from 2010 through 2012 and held the position of head triathlon coach at Life Time Fitness, Inc., a publicly traded national health club chain.

Jacobson has been a competitive triathlete since 1988 and continues to compete at the elite masters level. In the 1990s he became a professional triathlete, winning several USA Triathlon Long Course National Championships and placing as high as 20th overall at the Ironman Triathlon World Championships. For more information, visit his website at www.coachtroy.com.